Dear Missionaries

Letters From A Mission President To Missionaries Of The Church Of Jesus Christ Of Latter-day Saints (The Mormons)

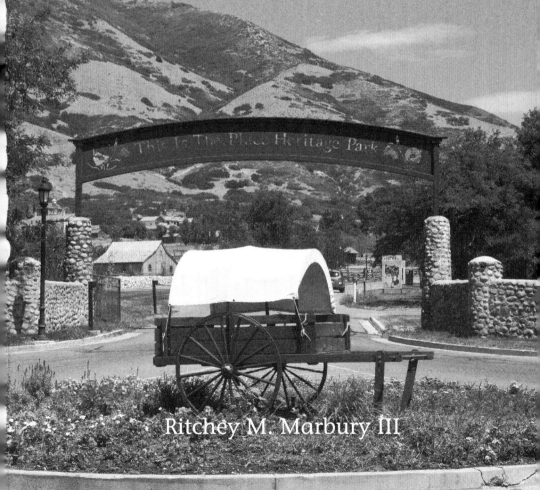

Ritchey M. Marbury III

Copyright © 2013 by Ritchey M. Marbury III

All rights reserved.

ISBN-10: 1481174207

EAN-13: 9781481174206

All images by Ritchey M. Marbury, III

This book is dedicated to the missionaries of the Church of Jesus Christ of Latter-day Saints—past, present, and future. It is also dedicated to the parents of those wonderful full-time missionaries as well as all who share the gospel with their family, friends, neighbors, and others with whom they have any influence or contact. Fonda (my wife of more than fifty years) and I love you all.

Dear Missionaries

Letters from a Mission President to Missionaries of the Church of Jesus Christ of Latter-day Saints (The Mormons)

Contents

Introduction	xi
Thirty-Five Years after Full-Time Mission	1
Act Your Best When Others Act Their Worst	6
American Atheists Say Mormons Are Dangerous	8
Are We Neighbors As Usual?	11
Attitude Determines Success	14
Be Faithful in the Little Things	16
Be Strong in the Hard Moments	18
Be the Best of Whatever You Are	19
Bible Teachings of the True Church	21
Bible Teachings Testify of the True Church	24
The Big Game	26
Bind the Lord	28
The Bride and the Vacuum	30
A Bright Christmas	32
Charity Is the Pure Love of Christ	35
Chinese Wise Man Lao-Tse	37
Chip Away the Evil to Find the Good	39
Christ Is Just a Prayer Away	41

Christmas Is a Time for Both Love and Action	44
Christmas Is for Giving	46
Christmas Means Love	48
Continue to Minister	51
Conviction Must Be Converted Into Conduct	53
Cotton and the Boll Weevil	54
Credit or Accomplishment	56
Dare to Be Uncommon	58
Decide Now and Act	60
Develop Purity	63
Do Good on Purpose	65
Do It	68
Do Many Good Things of My Own Free Will	70
Eight Conversion Factors	73
Endure to the End	76
Express Thanks	78
Faith–Purity–Action	79
Feed the Good, Starve the Evil	82
Five Basic Qualities for Missionary Success	85
Florence Chadwick—Catalina Channel	88
For God So Loved the World	90
Give More Praise	94
Give the Savior a Bright Christmas	96
Graceful Speech	98
The Habit of Winning	100
A Harvest of Convert Baptisms	103
Harvesting and Gleaning	105
How We Act When No One Knows	107
I Can Do All Things through Christ	109
I Can Do More and I Will	111

Ideas from Missionaries at Zone Conference	113
"If—" by Rudyard Kipling	115
If You Want a Thing Bad Enough	117
I'll Go	119
In the Beginning God	121
It Can Be Done	124
Jeremy Bentham Syndrome	127
John Jacob Astor	129
Kindness Works	131
Let Not Your Hands Be Weak—Work	132
Lift Up Your Heads	134
Love and Sacrifice	135
Love, Faith, and Personal Commitment	138
Love Is the Key to Life	141
Love One Another	143
Love Your Calling	145
Make a Zion Mission	147
Make Christ the Center of Your Life	149
Make Your Performance Match Your Potential	151
Making Friends	153
Many Great Leaders Were Once Called Failures	155
The Miracle of Faithfulness	157
Missionaries Are Teachers	159
My Missionary Commitment—Don't Quit	161
Neglect Not the Gift That Is in Thee	164
Nehemiah and the Wall	166
Night before Christmas, With Apologies	168
No One Goes Far Looking into the Rearview Mirror	170
Opportunity	172
Opportunity of a Lifetime and a Lifetime of Opportunity	174

Our Mission—Represent the Savior	176
Pay the Price	178
Perform One Successful Act Many Times	180
Persistence	183
Pick Up Your Sox	185
Plan Your Work	187
Power through Purity	190
Precise Obedience	192
Purity Includes Action	194
Put Away Childish Things	196
Put On Charity	198
Recharge Your Batteries	200
Remove the Mountain	201
Repeat Success, Correct Mistakes	202
Results Are According to Effort	204
Self-Denial	206
Self-Discipline Is a Key to Success	208
Serious Covenants Made to the Lord	210
Set Your Goals	212
Six Commitment Principles	214
The Spirit Knows No Handicap—First Thanksgiving	216
Spirit of Christmas	219
The Successful Never Give Up	221
The Sun and the Wind	223
Take the Lord's Side on Every Issue	225
The Teachings of Nephi	228
Tenth Anniversary of Our Baptism	230
That We May All Be One—A Student's Prayer	231
Think Uphill Thoughts	234
This Christmas, and Always, We Serve the Savior	235

This Christmas, Increase the Spirit of Love	237
Thomas and Henry Ward Beecher	239
Three Meetings	240
To All There Is a Season	242
Tribute to James Melvin Weaver	244
True Conversions	246
Truth Needs No Disguise	248
Turn Problems into Opportunities	250
Unselfish Service in the Animal Kingdom	252
Unwavering Standards	254
The Urgency of Doing	256
Use Time to the Lord's Advantage	257
When In Doubt—Pray	259
Where Shall I Work Today?	261
Will You Give Up What You Are to Become What You Can Be?	263
The Word Is Urgency	265
Yes Virginia, There Is a Santa Claus	268
Final Letter from Mission President to Full-Time Missionaries	271
Final Letter from Mission President to Stake Missionaries	273

Introduction

My wife and I served as mission president and companion in the Idaho Pocatello and Idaho Boise Missions from July 1978 through June 1981. We were called to serve in the Idaho Pocatello Mission starting in July 1978. In July 1979 the mission headquarters was moved from Pocatello, Idaho, to Boise, Idaho, and the mission name was changed to Idaho Boise Mission. During our three years of service, I wrote a weekly letter to the full-time missionaries and a monthly letter to the stake and ward missionary leaders. Some have requested these letters be published in a book so that they would be available for reading and, perhaps, be an inspiration to other missionaries—past, present, and future. This collection of many of the letters is in answer to that request.

The purpose of the letters was to inspire and motivate both full-time missionaries and all members. Some minor editing has been done to correct grammar, spelling, and so that the letters will be as fitting to all members and missionaries as they were to the missionaries serving with us in the Idaho Pocatello and Idaho Boise Missions.

These letters are filled with stories, poems, anecdotes, and quotations that teach valuable lessons to those who understand the blessings that come with missionary service. Many of the ideas were not original, but rather conceived by others and believed to be helpful in strengthening testimonies and motivating others to useful action. Where ideas were found to meet these criteria, they were included in the letters sent to the missionaries. A few photographs taken by us of sites along the Mormon Trail are also included for the enjoyment of the reader.

Dear Missionaries

May the Lord bless all who read these many letters in order to increase their love for our Heavenly Father and His Son Jesus Christ. May you all not only enjoy the letters, but also increase your commitment to share the gospel of the Restored Church with all those with whom you have influence.

Love,
Ritchey and Fonda Marbury

Thirty-Five Years After Full Time Mission

Dear Missionaries,

Fonda (my wife of more than fifty years) and I think often of the wonderful times more than thirty-five years ago when we were first called to serve full time as mission president and companion for the Church of Jesus Christ of Latter-day Saints. We know today as we knew then that God lives, that He loves us, and that The Church of Jesus Christ of Latter-day Saints teaches us the truth about how to be happy both now and throughout the eternities.

For those with whom we had the privilege of serving then, for the many serving now, and for any others choosing to read this book, here are some of our thoughts today—some thirty-five years after our full-time service:

- Jesus Christ is always our example and role model. We make a significant difference for good when we model Christlike behavior at all times.
- When we focus on love and charity, we focus on the greatest of all virtues.
- When we look for the good, we will find it; and isn't that what we really want to find?

Dear Missionaries

– Our Heavenly Father's commandments are given to us as gifts and may also be defined as "guidelines for happiness."

Here is a sonnet I wrote that expresses some of my thoughts in verse. It is included here hoping that it will motivate and inspire.

When

When we can fill our hearts with charity
And love our neighbors as we love ourselves.
When we can speak with truth and clarity
While others simply brag about themselves.

When we can hear some gossip and abstain
From gossiping ourselves or acting coy.
When we can help those hurting to regain
Some happiness and, once again, some joy.

When we can all forget and all forgive
The wrongs and hurts we get, although unjust.
When we can think about the way we live
With few regrets and many friends we trust.

We all will be at peace and all shall see
How wonderful a world that this can be.

Fonda and I love you all and miss the many fun and spiritual experiences we had so many years ago. May all of us continue to be missionaries in our thoughts, words, and especially our actions I pray in the name of Jesus Christ.

Love,

Ritchey and Fonda Marbury

Thirty-Five Years After Full Time Mission

*"Never judge, and always keep in mind
The smartest way to act is just be kind."*

—Ritchey Marbury

THE SACRED GROVE – PALMYRA, NEW YORK

Act Your Best When Others Act Their Worst

Dear Missionaries,

"Bear ye one another's burdens, and so fulfill the law of Christ." (Galatians 6:2)

You are servants of the Lord, divinely called upon and set apart to represent Him in all things. You are called to do the things Christ would do if He stood in your place. You are called to live the laws of love, obedience, and sacrifice.

Being Christlike begins with your relationships with your companion and fellow missionaries. It begins with you living the laws of love regardless of how others may act. Do you object to how your companion treats you? Then treat him or her as you wish to be treated. Do you feel some leaders exercise unrighteous dominion? Then serve them with even greater zeal so that your loyalty might serve to strengthen their love and humility. Do you feel you should be respected more as a leader? Then be a more diligent servant. When others act their worst, you are called upon to act your best.

You are called to baptize and blessed with power from on high to succeed. Companionships can baptize many more each month. We will reach the harvest through individual purity.

You are celestial missionaries. Like me, however, you have enough weaknesses to keep you all humble. Through humility, obedience, and faith, you will gain the power to move the mountain. My wife and I love each of you deeply. We pray daily that you will succeed in harvesting many souls, including your own. We know you will.

>Love,
>
>President Marbury

"When others act their worst, I will act my best."

AMERICAN ATHEISTS SAY MORMONS ARE DANGEROUS

Dear Missionaries,

In the April 19, 1981, issue of the *Idaho Statesman*, Madalyn Murray O'Hair, national president of the American Atheists Organization, was quoted as saying that the Mormons are "the single most dangerous religion in the United States." Coming from one who leads an organization dedicated to destroying a nation's belief in Jesus Christ and our Heavenly Father, this is a compliment.

I'm grateful to be part of a church that is considered dangerous to those openly opposed to God, Christ, prayer, and eternal salvation.

I'm grateful to be part of a church that knows what it believes and is not ashamed to tell the world. I'm grateful we declare with firm conviction that Jesus is the Christ and is alive today. I'm glad we know the difference between morality and immorality, between proper marital intimacies and sexual promiscuity, between uplifting literature and pornography.

I'm grateful to be part of a church that sets high standards, that teaches us to develop habits of purity, that insists on good works as well as the avoidance of evil, and that encourages self-discipline, obedience, and sacrifice for righteous causes. I'm thankful those standards include healthy living, that we understand the body is a temple not to be defiled by alcohol, tobacco, or other harmful substances. Because of the Church, I have learned that to make the difference, we must do things differently. I have learned that like an echo, what we do, good or bad, comes back to us.

I'm grateful to be part of a church that believes in work; that deplores the dole; that teaches that idleness is a curse; and that assists its needy through education and job opportunities, thereby maintaining their self-respect while helping provide them with the necessities of life.

I'm grateful to be part of a church that declares that families are forever, that teaches that "the greatest work we will ever do will be within the walls of our own home," that understands that "no success can compensate for failure in the home," and that explains how husbands and wives and their children can continue their close family relationships throughout the eternities.

I'm grateful to be part of a church that teaches positive attitude, that teaches us to be peacemakers rather than ones who create contention. Happiness is a habit, and the Church teaches us how to cultivate it. Unhappiness is a disease. Chronic unhappiness is bad manners, and the Church provides a cure for both.

I'm grateful to be part of a missionary church. We know that God lives, that Jesus is the Christ, and that God speaks to men today through living prophets. We know that we are literally the sons and daughters of God, and we love all people enough to dedicate our time, money, and resources to the end of sharing this same knowledge with others.

I'm grateful to be called a Latter-day Saint. I'm far from perfect, but I'm striving for perfection. I care. I want to do what is right. I understand that the word *saint* doesn't mean that I'm without fault, but that I'm striving to perfect myself. I love the Lord. I love my Heavenly Father, and I love all people. You lift me. I'll lift you, and we'll ascend together as one eternal family.

>Love,
>
>President Marbury

"Develop habits of purity."

Are We Neighbors As Usual?

Dear Missionaries,

In his opening address to the Sesquicentennial Conference, President Spencer W. Kimball, in referring to missionary work, asked, "...Are some of us still being 'neighbors as usual,' not yet fully sharing the gospel with our friends and neighbors?"

Elder M. Russell Ballard during the priesthood session of that same conference asked attendees to "let me show how each of us can make a sincere and meaningful commitment to Heavenly Father right now. Write...the name of one inactive or nonmember man or boy who lives in your ward. Will you make a commitment tonight that you will do all in your power, with the help of the Lord, to lead that person out of darkness into the full light of the Gospel?"

Our Heavenly Father measures our love for Him by how well we obey Him in following the council of His prophets and leaders. We have the counsel. What will be our response?

We are at war with the forces of evil. Satan reigns over evil. Christ reigns over good. We represent Christ at the frontline of the battlefield. As His soldiers, we commit ourselves to be the following.

TRUSTWORTHY

To be trustworthy means to be worthy of confidence; it means to be dependable. Some people cannot do what they are told.

Others do only what they are told. Neither of these are worthy of the Lord's full trust. Trustworthy soldiers in the Lord's army will do precisely what Christ would do were He present. They will be valiant. They will prefer the right road to the easy road. They know that following the path of least resistance makes men, women, and rivers go crooked.

Trustworthy soldiers are prayerful soldiers. They know that although sin may keep one from prayer, prayer will keep one from sin. They pray for missionary experiences daily, and after making this request through prayer, work diligently to assist in this request being granted.

WELL DISCIPLINED

Trustworthy soldiers in Christ's Army discipline themselves to the point that they know what to do and do it. They accept responsibility for their own actions—whatever the consequences. They avoid making excuses or blaming others for their shortcomings. They do what is right simply because it is right.

Well-disciplined soldiers live according to an orderly pattern of behavior. They pattern their lives after that of Christ. They know the necessity of focusing on a righteous goal and getting themselves into spiritual condition to obtain it. They know how to keep their temper—nobody else wants it. They know that to hit the target, they must first pull the trigger. To succeed, they must exhibit the self-discipline to make the effort.

COMMITTED TO WINNING

The Lord is a winner. He picks winners to represent Him. In the battle for the souls of men and women, winning is the only acceptable outcome. Winners give their all to reach the objective. They know that people are not honored for what they receive, but for what they give. If at first they don't succeed, they're about normal. They simply must persist until they do succeed. The winner is an ordinary person with extraordinary determination.

Winners are full of enthusiasm. They are dedicated. They know that patience with mediocrity is often an excuse for a lack of dedication. Winners possess unwavering faith. They recognize that "doubts are traitors that make us lose the good we oft might win because we fear to attempt."

Each time we see others who are not members of the Church, and are pricked in our hearts to share the gospel with them, we are pitted in a battle with Satan. We lose the battle when we fail to approach them about the gospel. We win when we invite them into our homes to be taught by the missionaries.

The Scriptures teach us to declare the gospel "...upon the mountains, and upon every high place, and among every people that thou shalt be permitted to see" (D&C 19:29). If we see other people, we are instructed by the Lord to declare to them the good tidings of the gospel. As we do so, we win the battle with Satan. May we all be committed to winning the battle for the souls of men and women, I pray in the name of Jesus Christ. Amen.

Love,

President Marbury

"The winner is an ordinary person with extra ordinary determination."

Attitude Determines Success

Dear Missionaries,

Here is a poem I wrote some years ago about attitude and success. Hope you like it.

Attitude Determines Success

*One hundred thousand dollars now remained
From millions he had earned in years gone by.
Somewhere his business judgment went awry.
"I've failed, my life is over!" he complained.*

*Another hundred thousand found its way
Into a pauper's hand through quirk of fate.
With pride he strutted up to his good mate
Announcing, "I've attained success this day!"*

*One hundred thousand dollars each was worth
As on a ledge they paused to think and plan.
The first, a suicide, then jumped to Earth;
The latter went his way a wealthy man.*

Attitude Determines Success

The same wealth brings some comfort, some distress;
For attitude determines true success.

Love,

President Marbury

"Attitude determines altitude."

—Zig Ziglar

Be Faithful In The Little Things

Dear Missionaries,

"And he said unto him, 'Well, thou good servant: because thou hast been faithful in a very little, have thou authority over ten cities.'" (Luke 19:17)

Faithfulness in the little things, attention to detail, a willingness to do things precisely—these are the virtues that produce winners. Failing to do well in the little things often produces larger failures.

Some years ago the United States Congress passed a resolution that should have read "All foreign fruit-plants are free from duty." Yet the clerk mistakenly replaced the hyphen with a comma when publishing the resolution, causing it to read "All foreign fruit, plants are free from duty." That one misplaced comma cost the American government two million dollars before the error could be corrected by a new Congress.

In the bottom of the ninth inning of the September 8, 1908, National League baseball game between the New York Giants and the Chicago Cubs, the score was tied and the Giants had runners on first and third bases. The batter hit a single, and the runner on third scored. Fred Merkel, however, was on first, and when he saw the runner on third score, he stopped running before he reached second base and returned to the clubhouse. Johnny Evers of the Cubs retrieved the ball, touched second base, and Merkel was out. The winning run was nullified. Excited fans on the field made it impossible to complete the game that day, but when the game was finished on a later date, the Giants lost. They also lost the pennant.

Faithfulness in the very little things is a very big thing. The Lord is looking for leaders. He is seeking men and women who care enough to serve Him in even the smallest areas of personal activity. We are the Children of God, but He needs more adults. When committing members to have their friends taught in their homes, are we careful to uplift before we commit? Are we as careful to use the language of Deity in our apartment as we are in a teaching situation? Do we refrain from chewing gum in public? Do we remember to ask for the Lord's blessing in every teaching situation? By your daily actions you are working out your own salvation.

Love,

President Marbury

"In great matters men show themselves as they wish to be seen; in small matters as they are."

—GAMALIEL BRADFORD

BE STRONG IN THE HARD MOMENTS

Dear Missionaries,

    May each of you know how grateful I am for your love and dedication. I am sure the Savior is well pleased with your hard work. Many souls are entering the gate of eternal life through your diligence.
    Stephen R. Covey, in listing ten basic principles of effective missionary work, gives as the tenth principle "Be strong in the hard moments." He states that there are certain crucial moments in any human behavior that, if excellently used, become determining moments. These moments decide the course of future events.
    It is in the hard moments that our real service is performed. All that the Savior did was predicated on his atoning sacrifice. Much of our success will also depend upon our willingness to sacrifice. Can we sacrifice our tendency to express anger even when we are right and another wrong? Can we sacrifice our desire to judge, replacing it with love unfeigned? The crucial moments are often the hardest moments of our mission. May we show strength equal to the moment, I pray in the name of Jesus Christ. Amen.

                                    Love,

                                      President Marbury

"I will be strong in the hard moments."

Be The Best Of Whatever You Are

Dear Missionaries,

The other day I came across this poem by Douglas Malloch that states in a very good way an important message for all. I am including it in this letter in order that it may help you as it has helped many others.

Be the Best of Whatever You Are

If you can't be a pine on the top of the hill,
Be a scrub in the valley—but be
The best little scrub by the side of the rill;
Be a bush if you can't be a tree.

If you can't be a bush, be a bit of the grass,
Some highway happier make;
If you can't be a muskie, then just be a bass—
But the liveliest bass in the lake!

We can't all be captains; we've got to be crew,
There's something for all of us here,
There's big work to do, and there's lesser to do,
And the task you must do is the near.

Dear Missionaries

If you can't be a highway, then just be a trail,
If you can't be the sun, be a star;
It isn't by size that you win or you fail—
Be the best of whatever you are!

God bless you all.

    Love,

    President Marbury

"Be the best of whatever you are!"

—DOUGLAS MALLOCH

Bible Teachings Of The True Church

Dear Missionaries,

As we testify of gospel truths to our friends, we are fortunate that most of them already believe and accept the Bible as the Word of God. Sometimes it may be helpful to have them compare the teachings of the Bible with those truths taught by the Church of Jesus Christ of Latter-day Saints. As they find the two identical, they will come closer to an understanding of why this is the Lord's Church. With the aid of Elder Derek A. Cuthbert of the First Quorum of the Seventy, the following list has been prepared to help you do this.

BIBLE TEACHINGS OF THE CHURCH OF JESUS CHRIST

ORGANIZATION

Officers in Christ's Church:
- Apostles and prophets — Ephesians 2:19–21; Ephesians 4:11–13
- High priests — Hebrews 5:1, 8–10
- Seventies — Luke 10:1
- Elders — Acts 14:23; Titus 1:5
- Priests — Exodus 28:1; 40:15

Teachers, apostles, and prophets	1 Corinthians 12:28–29
Deacons and bishops	Philippians 1:1
Patriarchs	Hebrews 7:4; Acts 2:29
True priesthood authority	Hebrews 5:4
No paid ministry	1 Peter 5:2
Melchizedek priesthood	Hebrews 7:11–12, 17
Named after Jesus Christ	Ephesians 2:20
Members called *saints*	Ephesians 2:19
Not a majority Church	Matthew 7:13–14

PRINCIPAL BELIEFS

A personal God	Hebrews 1:1–3
We are the literal offspring of God	Acts 17:29
Three separate persons	Matthew 3:16–17
The divinity of Christ	John 14:6
Jesus as the mediator	1 Timothy 2:5
Continuous revelation	Amos 3:7
Additional scripture	Ezekiel 37:15–17
Physical resurrection of Jesus	Luke 24:39
Physical resurrection of man	Job 19:25–27
All shall be resurrected	1 Corinthians 15:19–22
Pre-existence	John 9:1–3, Jeremiah 1:5
Christ's visit to "other sheep"	John 10:16
Purposeful prayer	Matthew 6:5–8
Clean living	1 Corinthians 3:16–17
Good works essential	Matthew 16:26–27
	James 2:19–20
First principles	Acts 2:37–38
Authority to baptize necessary	Acts 19:1–6
Holy Ghost given by laying on of hands	Acts 19:1–6
Second coming of Christ	Matthew 24:36–44
Angel messengers	Revelation 14:6–7
Three degrees of glory	1 Corinthians 15:40–42
Payment of tithing	Malachi 3:8–10

Ordinances and Gifts

Baptism essential	John 3:5
Baptism by immersion	Matthew 3:16; John 3:23
Little children blessed, not baptized	Mark 10:13–16
Sacrament	Luke 22:19–20
Gifts of the spirit	1 Corinthians 12:1–11
	Mark 16:17–18
Baptism for the dead	1 Corinthians 15:29
Administration to the sick	James 5:14
Gift of the Holy Ghost	Acts 2:38; 19:1–6

As we teach and testify, may we fill every word with love unfeigned. The Church of Jesus Christ is a church of love for all. Knowledge shared with tenderness blesses both the giver and the receiver. God bless you as you share.

Love,

President Marbury

"The Spirit only communicates through tender feelings."

—Shawn Carmichael

Bible Teachings Testify Of The True Church

Dear Missionaries,

Often we are asked to show what the Bible says concerning the truths we teach. Here are some Scriptures you may like to use:

There is only one true church	Ephesians 4:5
There was an apostasy	2 Thessalonians 2:1–4
	Acts 3:19–21
	2 Timothy 4:3–4
Other Scriptures should be written	John 21:25
Man has seen God	John 6:46
	Genesis 32:30
	Exodus 24:9–11
	Exodus 33:11
Even the devils believe. Works, also, are essential.	James 2:19–20
We must be more than lukewarm Christians	Revelation 3:15–16
Prophets are needed in Christ's Church	Amos 3:7
	Ephesians 2:19–20

Bible Teachings Testify Of The True Church

The Sabbath is rightfully on the first day of the week	John 20:19
	Acts 20:7
Officers in Christ's Church:	
Apostles and prophets	Ephesians 2:19–21
High priests	Hebrews 5:1, 8–10
Seventies	Luke 10:1
Elders	Acts 14:23, Titus 1:5
Priests	Exodus 28:1, 40:15
Teachers, apostles, and prophets	1 Corinthians 12:27–28
Deacons and bishops	Philippians 1:1
Patriarchs	Hebrews 7:4, Acts 2:29

May the Lord bless you in your service.

Love,

President Marbury

"A horse can't pull while kicking; neither can a horse kick while pulling."

The Big Game

Dear Missionaries,

Many have asked for a copy of a story presented several zone conferences ago called "The Big Game." The author is unknown, but the message is one of inspiration. Here it is.

The Big Game

I am giving you the ball, son, and naming you quarterback on our family team, because the great referee is calling me out. I've been your coach, so I'll hand it to you straight.

There is only one game on our schedule, and that's the big game. It's going to last your whole life. What makes it seem a lot longer is that there is no timeout and no substitutes. You play the whole time without relief and you have to stay in there and take it, no matter how tough the going, until the final whistle blows.

You will have a great backfield to help you. They have won a wide reputation for dependability. Their names are faith, honesty, and charity. You will work behind a

The Big Game

powerful line. End to end it consists of loyalty, devotion, enthusiasm, self-respect, study, cleanliness, and good behavior.

Keep your eyes on those goalposts. They are the pearly gates. God is the referee and sole official. He makes the rules, and there is no appeal. There are ten rules. You know them as the Ten Commandments. You play them strictly according to the dictates of your own heart and conscience.

There is also an important ground rule. It is: As you would that men should do to you, do ye also unto them. In this game, if you lose the ball, you lose the game because you cannot score without the ball.

Now, here's the ball! It is your immortal soul. Hold onto it, son. Go in there and play your heart out! So long, big boy. I'll be watching that scoreboard!

May the Lord bless you wonderful missionaries to score high.

Love,

President Marbury

"Go in there and play your heart out. I'll be watching that scoreboard!"

Bind The Lord

Dear Missionaries,

When I was a small boy, I used to listen to a radio program entitled *Let's Pretend*. The program was about enchanted lands, faraway exotic places, and magical happenings. When the forces of evil would cast their spells over the good people of the village, it would appear that all hope was lost. Then, as if by magic, the heroes of the story would hear a voice from their fairy godmother telling them that if they would do some good deed, or be obedient to their hearts, the evil spell would be lifted. As the advice and counsel of the fairy godmother was followed, every hero's wish was granted. Good was triumphant. The forces of evil were defeated, and they all lived happily ever after.

As the forces of evil work on the people around us today, it may sometimes seem that all hope is lost. As we read the Scriptures, however, we may hear the voice of the Lord speaking to us as the godmother did in the fairy tales. The Lord says "I, the Lord, am bound when ye do what I say; but when ye do not what I say, ye have no promise" (D&C 82:10). As we follow the advice and counsel of the Lord, we bind Him to grant us success. We first make ourselves pure. Follow the Missionary Handbook. We then follow the proselytizing programs that we have been taught, particularly Lacing Together, the Positive Member Missionary Program, and the Transition Discussion. Members are asked to follow the prophet's council to prayerfully select a nonmember family to friendship and then friendship the family and invite them to be taught by the missionaries. When we do this, success is assured. Bind the Lord. He always keeps His promises.

                        Love,

                        President Marbury

"Those busy doing the Lord's work have no time to argue over His plans."

The Bride And The Vacuum

Dear Missionaries,

A young bride, anxious to have her home immaculate upon her groom's arrival after his day's work, purchased a new vacuum cleaner. It was reported to be the best on the market. She quickly assembled it and began cleaning. One hour and three rooms later, the home was no cleaner and she was much meaner. Infuriated, she dashed to another store, purchased a poorer quality cleaner, sold her original one for half price, and cleaned the house for the remainder of the day. When her groom arrived home, she spent the rest of the evening complaining about the inferior vacuum she had originally purchased.

In actuality, the original vacuum worked very well. She had simply attached the hose to the blower end rather than the suction end. Her hasty judgment caused her to lose half the money she spent on the original vacuum and end up with one of inferior quality. She was guilty of downgrading the product simply because she failed to use it correctly.

Others judge the gospel by the way it is used by those who profess to accept it. In other words, our actions provide the basis on which our investigators judge the value of our message. If our message is judged to be of little value, if the gospel is judged to be untrue, it may be because we fail to live pure lives and because we use what we know in an improper manner.

We have the best product in the universe—the true gospel of Jesus Christ. As we use it correctly by living purely, others will see its value and desire it for themselves. May we help them to obtain it, I pray in the name of Jesus Christ. Amen.

Love,

President Marbury

"He does not believe who does not live according to his belief."

—Thomas Fuller

A Bright Christmas

Dear Missionaries,

What would you do for a friend who devoted his entire life to making yours happier? How devoted would you be to a friend who left a home of luxury and ease to dedicate thirty-three years of his life entirely to you? If this friend paid all of your debts—past, present, and future—would you love him? If this friend made arrangements for you to live a perfect existence with him in mansions he prepared for you, would you be forever grateful to him? Would you want to make Christmas special for him?

Throughout the world we honor this special friend in December. We have parties; we prepare feasts; we sing songs; we play games; we give gifts. In short, we do many things to enrich ourselves and those closest to us. Who is the special friend? What can we do to make him happy?

OUR GIFT TO THE SAVIOR—A BRIGHT CHRISTMAS

This special friend is Jesus Christ. This Christmas we can give him no greater gift than loving a family into baptism. There is great joy in Heaven over all that repent, "and the first fruits of repentance is baptism" (Moroni 8:25). Church leaders have asked that we greatly increase our friendshipping activities, which in turn will greatly increase our convert baptisms. Every member family has been asked to friendship another family into the church each year. After Christ's gift to us, can we do less for him?

Let's give Christ a Bright Christmas. Let's give him thousands of bright faces all over the nation smiling at our newly baptized friends. Let's give him bright and cheerful voices declaring optimistically, "It can be done and we will do it!" Let's give him a bright attitude saying that we will "work with a will!" Let's give Christ a light that shines so brightly that our good works will glorify our Father in Heaven.

BRIGHTEN OUR ATTITUDE

We give Christ a Bright Christmas as we develop within ourselves a bright attitude. My wife used to often wear a charm bracelet that later went to our daughter on her sixteenth birthday. One of the charms was a small golden boxing glove with the notation "Heavyweight Champion, 1931." This golden glove was won by my father, who was knocked out of the ring by his opponent in the first two rounds of the golden glove championship fight, before he finally scored a technical knockout in the closing seconds of the third round. If this doesn't show the positive results of a bright attitude, note this additional fact: when my father won that bout against the existing heavyweight champion, he weighed only 135 pounds.

Zig Ziglar has said that attitude, not aptitude, determines altitude. The fatalist complains about the holes in his shoes while those busy serving the Lord say they are now "back on their feet." The Lord's anointed take action. The mediocre take a seat. Those with a celestial attitude see a glass of water and say it's half full. The pessimist observes the same glass and says it's half empty.

BRIGHTEN OUR ACTIONS

Someone said, "Work will win, when wishy-washy wishing won't." Others have stated that those who say it can't be done had better get out of the way of those doing it. Bright attitudes lead to bright action. Faith is demonstrated by works. Success is simple:

work hard, play hard, and believe. Failure is equally simple: sit, complain, and doubt. We all know what will please the Savior. Let's give him the brightest Christmas ever.

Love,

President Marbury

"As my gift to Christ, today and forever, I will brighten my attitude and my actions."

Charity Is The Pure Love Of Christ

Dear Missionaries,

"But charity is the pure love of Christ, and it endureth forever; and whoso is found possessed of it at the last day, it shall be well with him." (Moroni 7:47)

The other day an elder appeared to have an unusually happy spirit. He was so visibly happy that a nearby visitor inquired as to the source of his happiness. "Nothing special," he replied. "I just feel very lucky to have the companion that I have. He always makes me feel important."

Isn't that what a mission is all about? To make others feel important? Isn't that what the Savior does for us? He teaches us that we are His brothers. He teaches that He came to earth to be the servant of all. If He, being a god, serves us, how should we treat each other?

I commend you for your righteous desires, your faithfulness, and your willingness to persist even when you feel down. I know things get depressing for you at times. I know that sometimes you continue to work only because of your love for the Savior and your love for us. We love you, too, and want you to know that you strengthen us with your love. Thanks for what you do. Thanks for being yourselves.

                        Love,

                        President Marbury

"Charity is the root of true virtue."

Chinese Wise Man Lao-Tse

Dear Missionaries,

Lao-Tse, a Chinese wise man of twenty-five centuries ago, said this:

> The reason why rivers and seas receive the homage of a hundred mountain streams is that they keep below them. Thus they are able to reign over all the mountain streams. So this sage, wishing to be above them, he putteth himself below them; wishing to be before them, he putteth himself behind them. Thus, though his place be above men, they do not feel his weight; though his place be before them, they do not count it an injury.

Christ gave these words years later:

> "...Ye know that the princes of the Gentiles exercise dominion over them, and they that are great exercise authority upon them. But it shall not be so among you: but whosoever will be great among you, let him be your minister; and whosoever will be chief among you, let him be your servant: even as the Son of Man came not to be ministered unto, but to minister, and to give his life a ransom for many." (Matthew 20:25-28)

Dear Missionaries

The meaning is clear. Great leaders are great servants. Those who would hold the highest positions must give the greatest service. Sacrifice is a part of it. Loving dedication to others is essential.

Thank you for the outstanding service you give. You are leaders in the Kingdom of God. Greater leadership comes with greater service. Go for greatness!

Love,

President Marbury

"And whosoever will be chief among you, let him be your servant."

—Matthew 20:27

Chip Away The Evil To Find The Good

Dear Missionaries,

"...Abhor that which is evil; cleave to that which is good." (Romans 12:9)

The story is told of a man whose home was near a large granite rock. The rock was massive, and there seemed to be no way to remove it from the property. Feeling that some type of sculpture would be more attractive than a piece of rock, the man carved an angel. His neighbors were amazed. It was the best likeness of an angel they had ever seen. How, his neighbors asked, did he do it? "It wasn't hard," he replied. "I just chipped away everything that didn't look like an angel."

You are missionaries, although you may have some traits that need chipping away. Laziness needs to be removed at times, as does anger, bitterness, selfishness, rebelliousness, and anything else that is not characteristic of the Lord's representatives. Free of those traits that belittle, you may be delighted with who you really are and what you can accomplish.

You are free to choose the kind of missionary you will be. Will you work to achieve your goals or wait to see what happens? Will you work to overcome your own problems or blame them on someone else? Will you continue to study or hope that your present knowledge will be sufficient? Will you pay the price to achieve or listen to the free advice of doubters? Will you be

Dear Missionaries

the master of your own attitude or be mastered by the negative attitudes of others? The choices are yours. God bless you to make the right ones.

Love,

President Marbury

"Wisdom is knowing what to do next; virtue is doing it."

—DAVID STARR JORDAN

Christ Is Just A Prayer Away

Dear Missionaries,

    May we reflect on a time nearly two thousand years ago. It is the first day of the week. A young woman named Mary approaches the tomb of a loved one just three days in the grave. Nearing the sepulcher, she weeps as she sees the entrance stone removed and the body of her loved one gone. As she looks into the sepulcher, her tear-stained eyes see two beings in white sitting where the body of her loved one had lain. She continues to weep, and they say to her, "Woman, why weepest thou?" Her reply: "Because they have taken away my Lord, and I know not where they have laid Him" (John 20:13).

    We rejoice in the rest of the story. We find comfort in the words, "…Why seek ye the living among the dead? He is not here, but is risen…" (Luke 24:5-6). Today no one should be able to say that they know not where to find Christ. No one needs to seek the living among the dead.

CHRIST IS JUST A PRAYER AWAY

    Christ lives and is just a prayer away. As we talk with our Heavenly Father in the quiet moments of our lives, we gain this sure knowledge. As we believe in the best, we find life.

None need say with Mary that they knows not where to find the Savior. Even as Mary wept, Jesus was standing beside her. He is with us also, and we find him among the living. We find Christ in the happy faces of little children as they bubble with gratitude at the small pieces of candy in the palms of their hands. We find Christ in the serene countenance of the sincere heart, kneeling in prayer at the beginning and end of each day. We find Christ beside the baptismal fonts, as repentant souls make His atonement effective in their lives. As we ask for any good thing with faith, in the name of Christ, we will receive it, if it is best for us.

JESUS IS A GOD OF SUCCESS

Jesus, speaking to his apostles after his resurrection, said "All power is given unto me in Heaven and in earth" (Matthew 28:18). Jesus is all-powerful. He is a God of success. Success is not promised until after the trial of our faith, but the final destiny of the faithful is success.

We often hear that the truth is learned by trial and error. However, we don't really learn by trial and error—we learn by trial and success. Christ's way is the successful way. After the trial of our faith comes the success of the faithful.

THE SAVIOR SUFFERED THAT BAPTISM MIGHT BE POSSIBLE

The last words of the resurrected Christ instructed his followers to teach and baptize. The atonement of Christ is only valid for those who repent of their sins and are baptized by proper authority. The admonition of the prophet is, "Do it now."

May we never be guilty of waiting to share our testimony with our friends and neighbors. May we never be guilty of saying to a soul striving to repent, "You'll have to wait a month or two before you can be baptized." May we always recognize that we will make mistakes that must be repented of daily. The repentant soul should be baptized now. If he or she hasn't completely repented today, help him or her to repent and be baptized tomorrow. It is our responsibility to help the perfection process—which begins with faith, repentance, and baptism—to start in every individual as quickly as possible. To do less is to allow the Savior to suffer in vain. That we might love enough to open the baptismal font as needed to those souls who, like ourselves, have many faults but are trying to overcome them, I pray in the name of Jesus Christ. Amen.

Love,

President Marbury

"After the trial of our faith comes the success of the faithful."

Christmas Is A Time For Both Love And Action

Dear Missionaries,

The Scriptures bless us by describing a number of events surrounding the birth of the Savior. It is interesting to note in these accounts the actions of the various people as they learn of the Savior's birth.

The obedient—depicted by the shepherds who were keeping watch over their flocks and doing what they should be doing—went in haste and found Christ. The wise—those so learned that the Scriptures simply refer to them as wise men—traveled a long distance to worship Him and bring gifts as soon as the signs appeared telling of His birth. The evil people of that day—as typified by Herod the King—simply sat, gave orders, and did nothing. Herod eventually grew so angry that he murdered little children throughout Bethlehem.

In the Book of Mormon we read of Nephi and others on the American continent at the first Christmas. They went forth baptizing the multitudes unto repentance. Christmas is not only a time for love but also a time for action, a time for missionary work, a time for convert baptisms. May the Lord bless you as you baptize and thereby follow the example set on that first Christmas.

>Love,

>President Marbury

"Christmas is not only a time for love but also a time for action."

Christmas Is For Giving

Dear Missionaries,

May I take this opportunity to express the thanks my wife and I have for all of you, each of you individually. We love you with all of our hearts.

Christmas is a time for sharing and giving. Like you, we are on a mission and can't give you many of the material things we would like to give. But there are things we can and do give you. Here are a few.

We give you our prayers. Neither a morning nor a night passes that we do not pray for you, for your happiness, for your success. We pray first that you will remain true to those principles that bring celestial exaltation. We pray that the Lord will watch over you and protect you from spiritual as well as physical harm. We pray that you will love the work here as much as you did the worldly fun back home. We pray for guidance to be the help and encouragement you need at the time you need it.

We give you our love. We love you as we love our own children. The most important things in our lives are you. We are happy when you are happy and feel sorrow when you feel sorrow. We always insist on the highest standards of performance, even when you may feel the standards are too high. When sometimes you fall below these standards, we correct you as best we know how, even though we know we risk your displeasure and perhaps even your anger. We love you that much. We do the same with our own children.

We give you ourselves. We seek only to serve you and the Savior. Our time is yours. Our hearts are yours. What knowledge we may have gained over the years we share with the hope that you will be enriched at least in some little manner. We are always available to serve and to help at any time you want us. You are our life. God bless you all.

Love,

President Marbury

"God bless you all. We love you."

Christmas Means Love

Dear Missionaries,

"For unto you is born this day in the city of David a Savior, which is Christ the Lord." (Luke 2:11)

Death is imminent! The ship is sinking! Flares are launched into the sky at regular intervals in hope that would-be saviors will see and respond. "Mayday! Mayday!" Radio broadcasts flood the airways.

The white flashes of light are spotted by the crew of the ocean liner Californian. No response. The flares are not recognized as distress signals. There can be no mistake about the radio messages, but there is still no response. The radio operator is sleeping soundly in his cabin. Only minutes away from the sinking vessel, providential guidance has provided a Savior ship. The Californian has halted its cruise this night in order to avoid oceanic ice, but it will not fulfill its errand of mercy. As some sleep and others fail to perceive the signs of distress, the crew of the Californian will sit idly by, unaware of the tragedy nine miles away—the sinking of the Titanic.

ARE WE AWAKE?

Parallels may easily be drawn between the sinking of the Titanic and ourselves. The Titanic represents those wonderful people around us who need the Savior and His restored gospel. The Californian represents the Savior and his restored gospel—nearby and divinely sent by Heavenly Father. The flares and radio messages are those acts, often angry and frustrated, with which others call attention to themselves—and which are in reality cries for help. We are the crew.

Although we easily spot the distress signals, we may not always understand. Other, plainer signals clearly indicate the need for help. If we are awake, we will hear the signals and take these people the restored gospel. If we remain asleep, they may perish.

CHRISTMAS MEANS LOVE

Christmas means love, joy, and happy times. In the warmth of our homes and with loved ones we share favorite stories and reminisce together. We exchange presents and cards as inadequate but sincere tokens of our affection for one another. Like a child with a new toy, we thrill at the snow and cold that on other occasions might solicit comments of a much gloomier nature. We love and are loved in return—because of the birth of one whose entire life meant love. He is a Savior to us. He asks us to be loving saviors to our neighbors.

SHARE THE GOSPEL

The gospel can't be kept by keeping it; it must be shared. Love is best gained by giving it away. We retain eternal blessings by sharing. This Christmas, while we are enjoying the love and fun the gospel affords us, might we not pause to listen to the cries for help from those whose happiness and salvation are drowning? Heavenly Father brings us frequently within the circles of influence of families struggling for eternal salvation. Christmas is a time to be especially attentive. The flares are launched. Will we recognize the signal? The distress message is being broadcast. Are we awake enough to hear?

Love,

President Marbury

> *"And now my beloved brethren, I have said these things unto you that I might awaken you to a sense of your duty to God."*
>
> —Alma 7:22

Continue To Minister

Dear Missionaries,

"I'm sure proud of you!" exclaimed the son to his father as they enjoyed each other's companionship at the ward picnic. The lad and his father sat together in two swings near the center of the park. The son was telling his father how proud he was of his father's missionary success in the ward.

"That family playing together throwing the Frisbee, you helped bring them into the Church, didn't you Dad?"

"I sure did, son. They accepted the gospel the first day they heard about it."

"And look at that girl helping prepare lunch. You taught her, too."

"That's right," replied the father. "The parents said they would disown her if she joined the Church, but there they are, helping their daughter prepare lunch. They told me the change in her was so dramatic they were glad she joined—even if they were against the whole thing at first."

As the father and son continued to reminisce, their gaze wandered to a remote area of the park where the lone figure of an older man stood motionless, looking down at the earth as though life were over while he was yet alive.

"You baptized him last night didn't you?" asked the son.

"Yes," replied the father, "but that's a sadder experience. After the baptism he told me his story. Ten years ago he came to our ward. He had a wife and two children then. I visited him once while he was being taught by the missionaries. He and his family wanted to be baptized, but he had a small drinking problem. He promised to quit and never drink again, but I told him he should wait a few weeks before being baptized so that he could prove himself. I was right in asking him to wait, but my failure was that I did not visit him again after that. He was not baptized until ten years later."

"'I could have quit my bad habits,' explained the convert. 'My family and I were committed to living the standards of the Church, but we were told to wait. No one would continue to work with us to help us live the standards until we were worthy to be baptized. I needed the strength of the stalwart members of the Church, but no one came. As time passed, I drank more and more—until I became an alcoholic. Eventually my family left me. I never saw them again.

"'Yes, I've finally accepted the gospel and become baptized— but I've lost my family! We could have made it together if only you had continued to love us, and help us, and work with us. Why did you quit visiting us? Why did you give up on us? Why?'"

The Lord taught us in 3 Nephi 18:32 "...for unto such shall ye continue to minister; for ye know not but what they will return and repent, and come unto me with full purpose of heart, and I shall heal them; and ye shall be the means of bringing salvation unto them." May we never give up on those the Lord has called upon us to bless. May we continue to minister unto those who do not yet seem ready to receive the gospel. We never know when we may be able to bless their lives and be the means of bringing salvation unto them.

Love,

President Marbury

"Continue to minister."

Conviction Must Be Converted Into Conduct

Dear Missionaries,

Thomas Carlyle said, "Conviction is worthless unless it is converted into conduct." That, to me, seems to be another way of saying that we show our convictions by our conduct. The way we act reveals our true feelings. Those things of most importance to us, we do. Those things of least importance to us, we fail to do. By our present actions, what are we telling the world is most important to us?

Love,

President Marbury

"Conviction is worthless unless it is converted into conduct."

—Thomas Carlyle

Cotton And The Boll Weevil

Dear Missionaries,

"And we know that all things work together for good to them that love God." (Romans 8:28)

Near the beginning of the twentieth century, a devastating plague swept across Alabama, particularly Enterprise, Alabama. The boll weevil, archenemy of cotton crops, ate its way through thousands of what at that time was considered to be the white gold of Alabama. With the destruction of the cotton crop, the economy of Alabama was virtually destroyed—at least, so believed the faint heart.

While some sold their farms and moved, others took faith in the promise given in the above scripture. They looked for another crop—a more stable and perhaps even more profitable crop. Instead of planting cotton, farmers turned to peanuts. The ensuing years proved the validity of how what appears to be a disaster can work to produce good. Alabama farmers reached new heights of prosperity, heights that would not have been possible from a purely cotton-based economy. In appreciation of their new prosperity, the people of Alabama erected a statue. It stands today prominently displayed in Enterprise Alabama, a magnificent monument to one of Alabama's greatest benefactors—the boll weevil!

Think for a moment about the boll weevil in your life. Maybe it's poor health. Perhaps it's the negative attitude of the local people toward you, or maybe it's simply that your investigators refused to commit. How can you make these difficulties work for good? There is always a way. Poor health usually helps you gain humility. When others show a negative attitude toward you, you can change their attitude by improving the way you act toward them. If your present investigators are slow to commit, success may come as you search harder for new investigators and improve committing skills. Learn from the past, but look to the future for new horizons of service. As you love God, all things will work together for good.

Love,

President Marbury

"And we know that all things work together for good to them that love God."

—Romans 8:28

Credit or Accomplishment

Dear Missionaries,

Concerning credit for deeds done, the Savior counseled, "But when thou doest alms, let not thy left hand know what thy right hand doeth: That thine alms may be in secret: and thy Father which seeth in secret himself shall reward thee openly" (Matthew 6:3–4).

Isn't it amazing how much good you can do when you don't care who gets the credit? The inventor of the hemocentrifuge, a centrifuge capable of separating blood cells from blood plasma, was such a person. His two later inventions are even better known and perhaps of even greater importance—the artificial heart and lung. This inventor's interest in medical research began when he flew a supply of pneumonia serum from the Rockefeller Institute to Quebec to save the life of a friend. Two years later he joined the staff of the Rockefeller Institute to begin research on what eventually led to the inventions of his life-saving devices. Since he always worked in secret, you probably never heard his name mentioned in connection with them. He was rewarded openly, however. He received the Pulitzer Prize some fifteen years later, although not for medical research, but for a book about another exceptional feat. His book—*The Spirit of St. Lewis*. His name—Charles Lindberg.

Credit Or Accomplishment

Are we working for credit or accomplishment? The glory of today is paper. The honor of eternity is gold. May your tomorrows be golden!

Love,

President Marbury

"Are we working for credit or accomplishment?"

Dare To Be Uncommon

Dear Missionaries,

Prior to a recent joint zone conference, I read an article written by Dean Alfange on our right to be uncommon. I would like to repeat his words to you here.

"I do not choose to be a common man. It is my right to be uncommon. I seek opportunity to develop whatever talents God has given me—not security. I do not wish to be a kept citizen humbled and dulled by having the state look after me. I want to take the calculated risk; to dream and to build, to fail and to succeed. I refuse to barter incentive for a dole. I prefer the challenges of life to the guaranteed existence; the thrill of fulfillment to the stale calm of utopia. I will not trade freedom for beneficence nor my dignity for a handout. I will never cower before any earthly master nor bend to any threat. It is my heritage to stand erect, proud and unafraid; to think and act for myself; to enjoy the benefits of my creations; and to face the world boldly and say, "this, with God's help, I have done."

Dare To Be Uncommon

May the Lord help you all to be so uncommon you do what those of lesser faith and perseverance would claim to be impossible.

Love,

President Marbury

"Dare to be uncommon."

Decide Now And Act

Dear Missionaries,

"It is ever the man who believes in his own idea; who can think and act without a crowd to back him; who is not afraid to stand alone; who is bold, original, resourceful; who has the courage to go where others have never been, to do what others have never done, that accomplishes things, that leaves his mark on time." (Orison S. Marden)

Here are some suggestions for the coming New Year to help you leave your mark on time.

BE A GOODFINDER, NOT A FAULTFINDER

Praise more. Criticize less. It is people with these traits that we enjoy being around. We like to be uplifted. We like being recognized for our good qualities. We are very much aware of our faults and would just as soon forget them. We need praise, and we especially like those who praise us when we least deserve it, because that is when we need it the most. It takes no more effort to see the good than to see the bad. We simply see what we look for. Beginning now, why not resolve to consciously look for the good things in life? You'll be happier—and so will all those around you.

BE PLEASANT, NOT BITTER

Act happy. Practice being pleasant. Forget petty grudges. Grudges are enemies to personal happiness. Concentrate on being grateful for the good things in life. After all, life is too short and too precious to waste on negative thinking.

Two men stopped to purchase a newspaper at a local newsstand. The attendant abruptly handed them the paper and waited impatiently as the men fumbled to find the correct change. Finally paid, the attendant berated his customers with vile and abusive language for keeping him waiting when he had other important things to do. The older of the two men smiled, apologized, and continued on his way.

"Why treat a man like that so kindly?" asked the younger.

"Because," came the reply, "I choose to be pleasant, and I'm not going to let someone whose behavior I dislike determine the way I act."

BE SUPPORTIVE, NOT CRITICAL

The Lord speaks to us in Doctrine and Covenants 1:38, saying, "...Whether by mine own voice or by the voice of my servants, it is the same." We read in 1 Samuel 26:9, "...For who can stretch forth his hand against the Lord's anointed and be guiltless?" One measure of your faith and worthiness before the Lord is your support of your Church Leaders. They represent the Lord. They are the Lord's anointed. If you would be faithful to the Lord, be supportive of His representatives.

MAKE PROGRESS, NOT EXCUSES

You can control your own destiny. Do you use a mirror or a telescope when seeking the reason for the results of your actions? Some use the excuse that they fail to keep the commandments because they fail to understand the Scriptures. The trouble is not in following those Scriptures they don't understand; it is in following those Scriptures they do. Julia Ward Howe once asked a senator to help a needy individual. The senator replied with the excuse that he was a busy man and had no time for individuals. Her reply was classic: "How interesting, not even God Himself is that busy."

Individual progress is up to the individual. Study and learn; fail to study and fail to learn. Work and achieve; fail to work and fail to achieve. Obey and receive blessings; fail to obey and fail to receive blessings. Treat others kindly and they'll treat you kindly; treat others unkindly and..."As ye sow, that shall ye also reap."

DO IT NOW

Decide now—and act. Failure to decide is a decision not to act. Often a poor decision to do something is better than no decision, which always results in doing nothing. Great souls act. Loving another into the Kingdom of God is one of the greatest acts you can perform. Resolve this year to have a family taught the gospel in your home. Do it now, so you can say it is done before failure says it's too late.

Love,

President Marbury

"I do not believe in a fate that falls on men however they act, but I do believe in a fate that falls on them unless they act."

—G. K. CHESTERTON

DEVELOP PURITY

Dear Missionaries,

Thank you for your many letters on ways to uplift the mission. Of all the ideas and suggestions, the most frequent was to help the mission developed purity. You are right. We are all here to grow spiritually and to help our brothers and sisters do the same. We must all remember that we represent the Savior. It is He that we labor for, and it is He who has called us. He will be our judge.

Purity comes by living the commandments with exactness—the small commandments as well as the more obvious ones. Christ teaches us to be in the world but not of the world. It therefore follows that our example should be above reproach. Our dress should be proper, especially at sacrament and other Church meetings. We should arise on time, cease from backbiting, work hard, and declare glad tidings. Our minds should think constantly of service to the Savior. All of you know the Savior's requirements to missionaries concerning TV, radio, tapes, reading material, etc. We show our love for the Savior by how well we keep His commandments.

Dear Missionaries

Today is the first day of the rest of our lives. May we begin anew to develop purity and demonstrate our love for the Savior.

Love,

President Marbury

"Seeing ye have purified your souls in obeying the truth through the spirit unto unfeigned love of the brethren, see that ye love one another with a pure heart fervently:"

—I Peter 1:22

Do Good On Purpose

Dear Missionaries,

Your challenge to Go for Greatness has begun. As only one percent of the membership loves another into the church each month, you will reach that destiny. Shall we begin now?

DEVELOP A WORKING LOVE

A desire is only a wish until the goal desired is written down and acted upon. Perhaps each Church leader could write down now, "My people will increase their membership more than one percent monthly through convert baptisms." There is magic in making big plans. Big plans stir the soul. Big plans require faith. They require action. They require dedication. They require us to purify our lives and become valiant enough to draw upon the powers of Heaven. Do you want to witness a miracle? Begin now to act on your righteous desires.

REPLACE WISHES WITH DESIRE

President Kimball has expressed his desire for every member to love someone into the church each year. He will be so pleased when you do it. Our sharing of the gospel with others expresses to our prophet our love and respect for his leadership.

As long as your heart is right, you will receive the individual inspiration to bring your neighbors into the Lord's eternal family unit. We all began as one eternal family. We had goals, desires, and ambitions. We wanted to be like our Eternal Parents. In a Heavenly Counsel we voted for the plan that would allow us to become like them. We knew the risks. We knew that the plan had dangers. We knew that if we failed we would be forever separated from each other. Having faith, we voted to come to this earth to be tested.

Departing the preexistent world of spirits must have been a sensitive moment for our Heavenly Parents. They loved us all dearly, and we loved them. As we arrived on this earth, many of us were blessed with the gospel. Others of our brothers and sisters were not.

Those who fail to accept the gospel may be separated forever from that family that loved one another so much before departing the world of spirits. Often I think I hear our Heavenly Parents crying over the possibility of being separating from one of their children. Sometimes I even think I hear them saying, "Your neighbors, don't you remember them? You were so close when you lived together as spirits. You will be so sad if you find yourself separated from them. Don't be too busy to love them. They loved you so much in the preexistence."

TAKE SPECIFIC ACTION NOW

The smallest righteous act is better than the greatest unimplemented plan. A little thing may be a little thing, but greatness is doing many little things well. Today, do some act of kindness for a neighbor. Today, tell someone not acquainted with the gospel how happy the gospel has made your life. Begin now to do something good—on purpose.

Now that you feel the joy associated with small acts of goodness, make some big plans. Big plans don't need to be complicated, but they will need to involve everyone doing something. That's what makes them big. Everyone Does Something. Keep records. No one fails who does even a small part, but help every member do something!

One of the easiest ways to involve everyone is through the Book of Mormon. Stake presidencies and bishoprics could begin by writing their testimonies in a copy of the Book of Mormon. They could include a family picture and give the book to the full-time missionaries to deliver to their friends. Later they could invite their friends to their homes for refreshments and to discuss what they have read. The full-time missionaries could be invited to help answer questions. A letter written by Ezra Taft Benson gives more details on preparing the Book of Mormon:

> Leaders are called to lead. The sheep will follow the shepherd. Once the example is set by stake presidencies and bishoprics, the rest of the membership will follow. The program is easy. It is recommended by the Church. It brings success.

My wife and I enjoy serving with you. We love it here and feel a part of you. We know you care. We love you. May the Lord bless you to lift others to the heights you have already attained, I pray in the name of Jesus Christ. Amen.

Love,

President Marbury

"I will act now to do good on purpose."

Do It

Dear Missionaries,

Several of you in our last interview answered, "I'll try," when committing to do several things. Bless your hearts; you all know that's not enough. You can do it. Perhaps this poem I wrote some time ago will encourage a more positive attitude:

Do It

His leg was pinned beneath the car.
The snow bit at his face.
His son was safe, without a scar,
Just cold, afraid. This place
Was fifty feet below the road
And he, a lad of ten,
Was told to leave this cold abode.
Climb out. Get help. Bring men.

With help nine miles down frozen trail
The son breathed out a sigh,
Gazed at the cliff he first must scale,
And told his dad, " I'll try."

Do It

Fearful, he went to climb the bluff.
His father called and said,
"Don't try my son, that's not enough.
Do it, or I'll be dead."

"I'll do my best!" the son explained,
His face determined now.
"That's not enough," his dad proclaimed,
"You do it son, somehow."
"I'll do it father," cried the son,
And up the cliff he braved.
Nine miles and back, the task was done.
His father's life was saved.

I've now resolved that I will dwell
On how I'll work steadfast,
Not how I'll "do my best," and fail,
Or "try," and finish last.
Though failure seems to lurk close by,
I'll still persist, somehow,
Then raise my head and firmly cry,
"I'll do it! This I vow."

May the Lord bless you as you "do it!"

Love,

President Marbury

"I'll do it! This I vow."

Do Many Good Things Of My Own Free Will

Dear Missionaries,

D&C 58:27 reads, "Verily I say, men should be anxiously engaged in a good cause, and do many things of their own free will, and bring to pass much righteousness." I am resolved to follow these words, this year and forever. Perhaps this five-step plan will help each of us.

1. I WILL PURSUE EXCELLENCE

I will not be satisfied with current standards of performance. There is a better way. I will not quit when I have done a good job. My work must be outstanding. I will do all that is required of me and more. I will never allow my goals to be simply what is required. I can do much more, and I will do it.

I will pursue excellence in every avenue of life. My speech will reflect a positive attitude and kind thoughts. I will live every requirement of my Heavenly Father. My professional life will also exhibit quality, for I know that religious zeal will not excuse mediocrity in any form. I will live with exactness, for I know that excellence means purity and exactness. In all that I do, I will go for greatness.

2. I WILL STUDY AND PREPARE MYSELF

I know that preparation and perspiration precede inspiration. I know that I will have opportunities to accomplish many things in life but that each individual opportunity comes but once. I know that my success in meeting each opportunity will depend on my previous preparation. I will therefore study each day so that when my time comes, I might be prepared.

I will not complain that my failures are due to bad luck. I know that luck is when preparation meets opportunity. I will prepare myself for consistent good luck. I know that one cannot fail who knows what to do and does it. I know that good memories must be arranged for in advance. I will not let a lack of knowledge rob me of potential blessings.

3. I WILL DECLARE GLAD TIDINGS

I am determined to maintain a cheerful countenance. I am committed to speak only the good. A cheerful attitude motivates both the giver and the receiver. A frown only dulls the senses to opportunity. I wish to uplift my acquaintances, to have those who associate with me feel enriched because of their association. I will search out the good and happy things of life and speak only of those things.

I will testify to all of the benefits of the gospel of Jesus Christ, for it is the most joyful truth I know. I will share the message that God lives and that Jesus is the Christ with boldness, but also with love. I will not allow fear to prevent me from sharing with others that which is most precious to me and which will bring eternal happiness to them. I will declare glad tidings.

4. I WILL BE MOTIVATED BY LOVE

I know that actions are the result of basic drives. Most of the drives revolve around self. These include self-preservation, security, reproduction, and recognition. The highest drive, however, is love, the pure love of Christ. When motivated by love, one forgets all personal or selfish desires in order to seek ways to benefit others. Love is an unconquerable force that will engulf any obstacle. Love is the most noble of all basic drives.

I know that true happiness comes only from service to others. I will develop my capacity to love to such an extent that I may serve without ceasing. I will not fail to love others simply because they fail to love me. I will love everyone that they might learn to love me and the message I represent. From this day forth, I will be motivated by love.

5. I WILL ENDURE TO THE END

I will persist until I reach success. I will never give up. I will work for those things that are required by my Heavenly Father and I will accomplish them. I know that no matter how seemingly impossible the task, a way will be prepared that it may be accomplished.

I know that the quitter always fails while success comes to those who endure. I know that faith, hard work, and endurance bring success. I shall develop these virtues. I shall discipline my will in order to develop mental toughness. I shall never fail, for I shall never quit. I will endure to the end.

Love,

President Marbury

"I will do many good things of my own free will."

Eight Conversion Factors

Dear Missionaries,

"Remember the worth of souls is great in the sight of God" (D&C 18:10). Our forefathers built a strong foundation for us in the Church. Today we have the opportunity to build on that foundation.

EIGHT FACTORS LEADING TO CONVERSION

A survey was taken of 1500 new converts of all ages in the United States and Canada to determine what factors led to conversion. It was discovered that conversion occurs in three phases: (1) gaining the investigator's interest (2) maintaining (3) conversion. Eight factors in each of these phases were found to be of prime significance. The relative importance of each factor, however, was according to the individual investigator's phase of conversion. These factors are listed below in the order of importance for each phase of conversion.

GAINING THE INVESTIGATOR'S INTEREST

1. Missionaries' testimony
2. Individual prayer
3. Missionaries' ability to teach and answer questions

4. The Book of Mormon
5. Member involvement
6. Meeting attendance
7. Activities with members
8. Personal feelings of the Spirit and observation of personal change

MAINTAINING

1. Individual prayer
2. The Book of Mormon
3. Member involvement
4. Missionaries' testimony
5. Meeting attendance
6. Activities with members
7. Missionaries' ability to teach and answer questions
8. Personal feelings of the Spirit and observation of personal change

CONVERSION

1. Individual prayer
2. Member involvement
3. Activities with members
4. Meeting attendance
5. Personal feelings of the Spirit and observation of personal change
6. The Book of Mormon
7. Missionaries' testimony
8. Missionaries' ability to teach and answer question

As you can see, although the ability of the missionaries to teach and answer questions is of high importance in the interest phase of conversion, actual conversion comes through individual prayer and member involvement. As we pray with our neighbors and become their friends, they will be converted and baptized.

I challenge all stake and ward leaders to achieve more member involvement with our nonmember friends. I challenge all stake and full-time missionaries to more effectively teach families to pray. I challenge every family to love another family into the church during the next twelve months. I challenge you to Go for Greatness!

Love,

President Marbury

"Remember, the worth of souls is great in the sight of God."

Endure To The End

Dear Missionaries,

"And, if you keep my commandments and endure to the end you shall have eternal life, which gift is the greatest of all the gifts of God." (D&C 14:7)

Enduring to the end is a virtue sometimes referred to as the fifth principle of the gospel. The first principle, we know, is faith in the Lord Jesus Christ. The second is repentance. Third is baptism, and fourth is the laying on of hands for the gift of the Holy Ghost. The blessings associated with the keeping of these principles, however, come only as we endure to the end.

In a few days, shortly after Christmas, this year ends. The last days of the year should yield our greatest efforts. "Winners never quit and quitters never win" is as true now as it ever was.

In the 1974 Kentucky Derby the first place winner defeated the horse in fourth place by only four seconds. The difference was $26,970. In another race in another place, a one inch lead over the second-place winner yielded a prize difference of $100,000. The efforts in the last seconds determined the winner.

The Lord loves those families we are teaching now. Why wait until next year for them to enjoy the benefits of the gospel? We are in competition with Satan for the souls of the people. Satan will end the year working hard. The Lord must win. As the Lord's servants we must end the year with our strongest efforts. Love hard. Work hard. Live pure. That's an unbeatable formula.

                Love,

                President Marbury

"Endure to the end."

Express Thanks

Dear Missionaries,

November is the month for thanksgiving. This month we will show our thanks to our Heavenly Father and His Son by helping to convert and baptize many souls into His Kingdom. The Savior desires many committed converts who will add to the strength of the wards and stakes.

Let us not be content with good when the best is within reach. You are chosen of God. You are chosen to reach heights never before reached by others. You will reach them in accordance with your faith and purity.

Begin this month with thanks. Write letters to your ward and stake leaders thanking them for all they do. Express thanks to your parents for the support they give you. And above all, express thanks to your Heavenly Parents for their love for you. "...With Thanksgiving let your requests be made known unto God" (Philippians 4:6).

May the Lord bless you to achieve greatness. My wife and I love each of you.

Love,

President Marbury

"Rub people the right way."

Faith—Purity—Action

Dear Missionaries,

I testify to you in the name of Jesus Christ that you can achieve happiness now and throughout eternity as you develop the virtues of faith, purity, and action.

FAITH

Someone once said, "Whether you think you can or think you can't, you're probably right." Christ said it this way, "If you have faith as a grain of mustard seed, ye shall say unto this mountain, remove hence to yonder place; and it shall remove; and nothing shall be impossible unto you" (Matthew 17:20).

We grow as we improve the way we think. Let us remove from our minds the idea that we have a problem and think instead that we have a challenge or an opportunity. Instead of thinking expense, think investment. Supposed failure is only the elimination of a temporary method of doing things so that a new and better method may be used. Replace "it can't be done and I quit" with "it can be done and I'll prove it."

PURITY

Love is the essential ingredient of purity. To be totally pure, become totally loving. Focusing on the salvation and the welfare of others removes all selfish desires from our hearts. Recognize that it is difficult to lift others to a degree of spirituality higher than our own. Also recognize that we can only be exalted to the level of our most serious personal sin. As we learn to love all people, we are better able to overcome our weakness and grow pure.

> I picked a bunch of roses that
> My friend might have a share,
> And when I came and looked again
> I found new rosebuds there.
> I think that they were saying,
> "Now don't you see it's true?
> When you give joy to someone else
> Much more comes back to you."
> —Author unknown.

ACTION

"If ye know these things, happy are ye if ye do them" (John 13:17). The key to success is action—doing what we know we can do. While we're doing, why not do more of that thing which is of most worth to us? The Lord has told us what it is in Doctrine and Covenants 15:6: "...bring souls unto me." He tells us to love our neighbors into the Church. If we doubt how important this is, this council is repeated in Doctrine and Covenants 16:6. A prophet of our Church, President Kimball, said to baptize thousands. Let's do it.

> Somebody said it couldn't be done,
> But he with a chuckle replied
> That maybe it couldn't, but he would be one
> Who wouldn't say so till he tried.
> So he buckled right in with a trace of a grin

Faith—Purity—Action

*On his face. If he worried, he hid it.
He started to sing, as he tackled the thing
That couldn't be done, and He Did It!*
—Author unknown

Those who say it can't be done had better get out of the way of those doing it. That we may be anxiously engaged in good works and endure to the end, I pray in the name of Jesus Christ. Amen.

Love,

President Marbury

"The key to success is action."

FEED THE GOOD, STARVE THE EVIL

Dear Missionaries,

The Duke of Wellington, perhaps the greatest field general of all time, was once asked what he would have done differently if he had his life to live over again. He replied, "I would have given more praise."

I, too, feel I haven't praised you enough for the love and service you have given to me and the Savior. A retention survey was completed for all convert baptisms from July 1979 through June 1980 in the Idaho Boise Mission. Your faithfulness resulted in 73.5 percent of all those baptized being active today. It is also interesting to note that 73.1 percent of those baptized were found by local members. Of all those converts called to a position in the ward, 95.3 percent are active today. The key to convert retention is clear—more local members finding investigators for the missionaries to teach and a greater emphasis on Church callings for all new converts. You are doing fabulous, and you can do even better.

FEED THE GOOD—STARVE THE EVIL

A small child takes its first step. As it attempts the next, it teeters and falls. Do we criticize it for falling—or do we praise it for the progress made in response to conscious effort? A young missionary baptizes several converts. Some have been well taught, others could have been taught better. Do we condemn the deficiency—or rejoice in the achievement?

A new convert attends a sacrament meeting. His clothes are not as appropriate as expected. Do we criticize the manner of dress—or express welcome, love, and acceptance for the conscious effort to attend the Lord's House?

Behavior is fed by the attention we give it. It is starved by ignoring it. As we attend to the good, we get good in return. As we attend to mistakes, we find mistakes increase. Blessed are those who do things unnoticed that contribute to the happiness of others. It's the little things no one else notices that God notices. Walk by the sides of those weaker than you until they can walk by themselves. Develop the love to find the good when all others are pointing out the bad.

COMMIT AND REPORT TO HEAVENLY FATHER

Suppose that tomorrow the First Presidency asked you to set a goal, commit to completing it that same day, and report your progress that evening. Would you complete it? You know you would. Suppose that instead of seeing the First Presidency, you simply pray for the Lord's help in reaching the same goal. Would you feel more committed to reaching the goal after talking with the First Presidency or after talking with the Lord? Be honest with yourself. How would you really feel? How should you feel? Those making a request through prayer are under divine obligation to assist in that prayer being answered.

May I suggest a daily habit for personal growth? Begin each morning with a prayer of commitment to Heavenly Father. Commit through prayer that you will perform a specific righteous act (you must be specific and tell the Lord exactly what that act will be) before retiring for the evening. Every evening report back through prayer your accomplishment. As you find yourself more committed to Heavenly Father than you would be if your commitment were made in person to the President of the Church, you will reach pinnacles of spirituality and personal growth worthy of celestial exaltation—pinnacles greater than ever previously imagined.

BE DILIGENT—AND BE KIND

While spanking his son, a father repeatedly explained that he was doing it because he loved him. The teary-eyed son answered that he could hardly wait to grow up so he could return his father's love. A better example of diligent kindness is found in the story of the lady who, observing a poor young girl admiring a new dress, purchased it for her and left without giving the child her name. Rushing to catch her benefactor, the child asked the lady if she were God's wife. "No," replied the lady, "Just one of His children." Approvingly the child remarked, "I knew you must be some relation!"

Voltaire said, "I know of no great men except those who have rendered great service." Often the good we would do, we don't do, because we don't think it. The greatest service we can render to others is to give them the restored gospel. The Savior said in D&C 15:6 that the thing of most worth to us is to bring souls unto Him. I testify to you that diligent kindness will bring results. I testify to you that great spiritual blessings accompany missionary work. May you receive these blessings, I pray in the name of Jesus Christ. Amen

Love,

President Marbury

"Feed the good—starve the evil."

Five Basic Qualities For Missionary Success

Dear Missionaries,

We all desire to be successful. I am convinced success comes through internalizing basic qualities. May I suggest five?

CHRISTLIKE SPIRIT

Paul explains in 1 Corinthians 13:8 that "Charity never faileth." Charity then, which is the pure love of Christ, becomes a guaranteed formula for success in anything. A Christlike spirit is the spirit of charity. Paul defines charity as long-suffering, kind, not guilty of envy, not puffed up, not guilty of behaving unseemly, not seeking her own, not easily provoked, not guilty of thinking evil, not guilty of rejoicing in iniquity, and rejoicing in the truth. Before every decision ask, "how would Christ act?," and act accordingly. A Christlike Spirit will take conscious effort to obtain, but the rewards are worth the effort.

SELF-DISCIPLINE

"He that hath no rule over his own spirit is like a city that is broken down, and without walls" (Proverbs 25:28). What time do we arise in the morning? Do we set aside a specific period of time each day for study and then study? Do we govern our lives by conscious effort or are we governed by circumstances that transpire at random? Do we do good things on purpose? Leaders of people are first leaders of themselves. To govern our circumstances in life, we must first govern our own actions. To discipline one's own life takes a rare form of courage. To do otherwise limits one forever to the mediocre.

WORTHWHILE GOALS

Where did we come from? Why are we here? Both are important questions. More significant are where are we going? Where do we want to go? What are our goals, and are they worthwhile? Will the attainment of our goals lead to eternal life? Scriptures teach us that "Jesus increased in wisdom and stature and in favor with God and man" (Luke 2:52). This gives us the key to the four basic areas in which to set goals: (1) educational, (2) physical, (3) spiritual and (4) social. A goal is more than a wish. A goal is the end toward which effort is directed—the specific determination of that which is desired and the direction of effort toward that desire. When the desire is a proper one, it brings success.

SPECIFIC PLANS

There is a difference between plans and specific plans. We may plan to work harder, study more, be a better missionary, and be more spiritual. These appear to be fine, but they are too general to be measured. Specific plans might be to begin work fifteen minutes earlier, study from 5:30 to 7:30 each morning, discuss the gospel with the Smith family today, and pray every morning and evening and before each meal. Our sincerity to do what we plan can often be determined by whether or not our plans are general or specific—and if they can be measured.

KNOWLEDGEABLE ACTION

Knowledge is potential power—not power, but potential power. It becomes power after it is put into action. Activity alone brings little benefit. There is a difference between activity and achievement, between busywork and accomplishment. Knowledge brings success only when it is coupled with action. Specific plans, prepared intelligently and implemented vigorously, achieve significant results.

With a Christlike spirit, self-discipline, and worthwhile goals—as you prepare specific plans and implement them with knowledgeable action—you'll succeed! God bless you to do so.

Love,

President Marbury

"Specific plans, prepared intelligently and implemented vigorously, achieve significant results."

Florence Chadwick—Catalina Channel

Dear Missionaries,

"And so, after he had patiently endured, he obtained the promise." (Hebrews 6:15)

My wife and I are so grateful for you. Each of you is an outstanding individual, capable of greatness as you overcome the little discouragements that fog your mind into believing you are less than you really are.

Florence Chadwick, the first woman to swim the Catalina Channel, failed in her first attempt because fog blocked her vision of the nearby goal. On July 4, 1952, she waded into the water off Catalina Island and began the twenty-one mile swim toward the California coast. The fog that day was so thick that she could barely see the boats traveling beside her to ensure her safety. For fifteen hours she swam with no sight of the California shoreline that would mark the end of her journey. She asked to be taken out of the water. Her trainer objected. Land was near. For a few more minutes she swam on, and then, after one hour and forty-five minutes, she quit. Only one half mile away was land. The fog had obscured her vision and her faith. Later she remarked to a reporter, "If I could have seen land, I might have made it."

Two months later, her determination and faith strengthened, she attempted the swim again; this time she made it. It was on another foggy day, but she swam with the assurance that somewhere behind that fog was the California coastline.

Never give up on any righteous endeavor. Most obstacles are far less potent than they appear when we are tired or discouraged, and often the goal is nearer than we realize. It has been said that a dense fog covering seven city blocks to a depth of one hundred feet contains only enough moisture to fill a single glass of water. When we reduce our problems to their real size, we find that their significance, like the seven blocks of fog, is not so much after all. You are called to succeed. Do it. The Lord is on your side.

Love,

President Marbury

"Every noble work is at first impossible."

—CARLYLE

FOR GOD SO LOVED THE WORLD

Dear Missionaries,

"For God so loved the world, that he gave his only begotten son, that whosoever believeth in him should not perish, but have everlasting life." (John 3:16)

You have done well this year. You have loved without ceasing. In this mission, of all baptisms last year, 72 percent are still active. Better yet, 98 percent of those converts baptized last year who were called to some position in the Church are still active. Because of the great team spirit among full-time missionaries and local members, true conversions are taking place.

The birth of Jesus Christ brought a new spirit into the world, a spirit of love unfeigned. It also brought a spirit of urgency. When the shepherds heard of the Savior's birth, Luke records, "And they came with haste" (Luke 2:16). When Jesus called his disciples, Matthew records, "And they straightway left their nets, and followed him" (Matthew 4:20).

The word at Christmas is "haste"; it is "straightway." In the words of President Kimball, the word is "urgency"—it is "now."

On the American continent, the first Christmas night was as bright as midday, and a new star appeared to announce the Savior's birth. It is recorded that Nephi and also many others went forth baptizing unto repentance. "And thus the people began again to have peace in the land" (3 Nephi 1:23).

The first Christmas in America was made sacred by an increase in missionary work and baptisms. Peace was restored to the land. This Christmas season can be equally sacred through the conversion of many souls. Let's do it!

Love,

President Marbury

"And they came with haste."

This particular letter to full-time and stake missionaries included a message from Elder Derek A. Cuthbert, one of the general authorities of the Church. That letter it included here:

Dear Fellow Harvesters,

You are to be commended for the thousands of gospel seeds you have sown and hundreds of souls you have harvested during this year, which is drawing to a close. How quickly the Lord brings an increase: "first the blade, then the ear, then the full corn shall appear." What a wonderful conversion process, from seed to ripened corn, and you have been fully part of this from doorstep testimony to baptismal ordinance. Congratulations, we are proud of you.

The Lord expects us to be "profitable servants":

to yield "an increase"
to "gather in the harvest."

He has entrusted us with a sacred stewardship. He has bestowed authority on us to preach the gospel and administer the ordinances thereof. All this that we might bring forth "fruit meet for [our] Father's kingdom" (D&C 84:58).

We thrill to hear of the way you are:

Overcoming adversity
Vanquishing the adversary and
Strengthening each other in the Lord's work.

"Fear not to do good, my sons, for whatsoever ye sow, that shall ye also reap" (D&C 6:33). The Lord expects each one of us to do our very best.

How true are the words of the Savior to his disciples: "The harvest truly is plenteous but the laborers are few" (Matthew 9:37-38). Almost a million of God's children live within the mission boundaries, and three out of four are not yet "in the strait and narrow way." We need many laborers to harvest such a plenteous harvest. "Pray ye therefore the Lord of harvest, that he will send forth laborers into his harvest." Yes, every member needs to be a missionary. This will double and triple the effectiveness of every full-time missionary.

The Psalmist proclaimed, "O Lord how manifold are thy works (Psalms 104:24). We need not only to redouble our efforts, but to bring forth a many fold harvest from our labors. President Kimball has declared in all solemnity, "Where we have been converting one soul, we can convert five!"

As we contemplate the field that is "white, all ready to harvest," as we picture in baptismal white the fine souls we are teaching, let us purify our thoughts, our words, our actions, so that we are pure and white and spotless before the Lord. It is a great privilege to be fellow harvesters with such fine dedicated missionaries who are striving "to keep [themselves] unspotted from the world" (James 1:27).

The Lord is adding to this kingdom, hour by hour, day by day, year by year, until that glorious day when He shall declare to His Father, "It is finished." At this season we celebrate the birth of our Lord Jesus Christ, the "lamb without blemish and without spot" (I Peter 1:19). He is our Redeemer, our Exemplar, our Mediator, our Savior. May we approach Him more nearly this Christmas time by being engaged with "heart, might, mind, and strength" in the sacred service of harvesting souls into His Kingdom. "And thus, if ye are faithful, ye shall be laden with many sheaves" (D&C 75:5).

May you have a happy, holy, harvesting, Christmas.

Sincerely Your Fellow Missionary,

Derek A. Cuthbert
Executive Administrator

"For God so loved the world that He gave His only begotten Son."

Give More Praise

Dear Missionaries,

The Duke of Wellington is perhaps the greatest field general of all time. Possibly no one can claim more victories than he. In the later years of his life, he was asked what he would have done differently if he had his life to live over again. Of all the answers he might have given, he replied thoughtfully, "I should have given more praise."

I share that same feeling. You are the finest missionaries in the world. You work harder, sacrifice more, and live purer than anyone I know. In the quest to reach our goals, the work you do is often not given the attention and praise it deserves. When you need correction, you are corrected, and this is right. That is how we all grow. Most often, however, you do things exactly the way they should be done. For my failure to recognize these achievements as often as I should, I apologize. Thanks for all you do for me and for the Lord.

Voltaire once said that he knew of no great men except those who have rendered great service. The greatest service we can render is to bring souls into the Kingdom of God through convert baptisms. You are doing a great service now as you continue to teach, testify, challenge, and baptize. God bless you all.

Love,

President Marbury

"Give more praise."

GIVE THE SAVIOR A BRIGHT CHRISTMAS

Dear Missionaries,

Welcome to the Christmas season, with all its food, fun, songs, and gifts. For many years we have honored the Savior with a white Christmas, and I'm sure he has been pleased. This year may we honor the Savior with a bright Christmas.

Let's give Christ bright faces all over the mission as they smile beside the waters of baptism. Let's give Him bright voices as we cheerfully declare with conviction, "It can be done, and we will do it!" Let's give Him a bright legacy while we firmly "work with a will." Let's let our light shine so brightly that our good works will glorify our Father in Heaven.

Brightness denotes cleanliness. No matter how powerful the source of light, it cannot give forth its full benefit until it is clean. Enough dirt and filth will darken even a flood light to a glimmer. The Lord said, "...yea, purify your hearts, and cleanse your hands and your feet before me, that I may make you clean" (D&C 88:74).

My wife and I love you all. We, too, are away from home and away from many of our friends and loved ones. We now direct all of our love to you. We desire with all of our hearts for each of you have a wonderful Christmas season. We know the Lord will bless you as you bless Him through total commitment. May we make this the brightest Christmas ever!

                Love,

                President Marbury

"Where love is, there God is."

Graceful Speech

Dear Missionaries,

"Let your speech be alway with grace, seasoned with salt, that ye may know how ye ought to answer every man." (Colossians 4:6)

Grace in our speech reveals polish, kindness, and a willingness to understand the other person's needs and concerns. Your listener, in turn, will be more willing to hear and act on your message. After all, it's not what we say that converts, but what is believed of what we say. As we teach with patience, we must be patient. As we teach understanding, we must understand. As we teach love, we must love. As we ask others to believe in us, we must believe in them.

Graceful speech expresses a positive attitude about one's surroundings and about the other person. In a study by a group of psychologists, students were divided into three groups and given negative, positive, and no feedback about themselves. They were then asked to play a game. The game was so arranged that each student would have several chances to cheat. The students who cheated most were the ones who received the negative feedback about themselves.

Others tend to do pretty much what is expected of them. Expect them to reject your message, and they will. Expect them to become converted and accept baptism, and they will.

As you teach grace, conviction, and a positive attitude, you will harvest.

Love,

President Marbury

"It's not what we say that converts, but what is believed of what we say."

The Habit Of Winning

Dear Missionaries,

This instruction by Vince Lombardi, one of football's greatest coaches, teaches a fundamental principle of success. It is entitled "The Habit of Winning."

> Winning is not a sometime thing. You don't win once in a while. You don't do things right once in a while. You do them right all the time.
>
> Winning is a habit. Unfortunately, so is losing. There is no room for second place. There is only one place in my game, and that is first place. I have finished second twice in my time at Green Bay, and I don't ever want to finish second again. There is a second-place bowl game—but it is a game for losers played by losers. It is and always has been an American zeal to be first in anything we do, and to win, and to win, and to win.
>
> Every time a football player goes out to play, he's got to play from the ground up. From the soles of his feet right up to his head. Every inch of him has to play. Some guys play with their heads. That's okay—you've got to be smart to be number one in my business. But, more important, you've got to play with your heart, with every fiber of your body. If

The Habit Of Winning

you are lucky enough to find a guy with a lot of head and a lot of heart, he's never going to come off the field second.

Running a football team is no different from running any other kind of organization—an army, a political party, a business. The problems are the same. The objective is to win—to beat the other guy. Maybe that sounds hard or cruel. I don't think it is.

It is a reality of life that men are competitive, and the most competitive games draw the most competitive teams. That's why they are there—to compete. They know the rules and the objectives when they get in the game. The objective is to win—fairly, squarely, decently, and by the rules—but to win. And in truth, I have never known a man worth his salt who, in the long run, deep down in his heart, didn't appreciate the grind—the discipline. There is something in good men that really yearns for...needs...discipline and the harsh reality of head-to-head combat.

I don't say these things because I believe in the "brute" nature of man or that men must be brutalized to be combative. I believe in God, and I believe in human decency. But I firmly believe that any man's finest hour, his greatest fulfillment to all he holds dear, is the moment when he has worked his heart out in a good cause and lies exhausted on the field of battle victorious.

Some have said this philosophy is too harsh, and that it is not whether you win or lose but how you play the game. That may be true, depending on how you define winning and losing. Remember, however, that even though some say that it is not whether you win or lose but how you play the game—they still keep score.

Remember also, that the Lord is the referee and scorekeeper in the game of life. He makes no bad calls, and He makes no mistakes. Also, the game of life is not a win–lose game. We can all be winners when we are obedient to the Lord's commandments, and the Lord's commandments are both the rules and the guidelines for happiness. In fact, in the Lord's dictionary, commandments are defined as "guidelines for happiness." In the game of life, we are all winners as we keep the Lord's "guidelines for happiness." May we all do so, I pray in the name of Jesus Christ. Amen.

Love,

President Marbury

"Keep the Lord's commandments—His guidelines for happiness—and win."

A Harvest Of Convert Baptisms

Dear Missionaries,

I'd like to take this opportunity to thank all of you for your excellence in working together and loving our friends into the Church. Missionary work is among the most rewarding of all Church service and, as stated in D&C 15:6, is the thing of most worth to us.

Like you, I have a great desire that we not only bring many souls into the Church, but also that they remain active. Beginning now, it is requested that all new converts have a friendshipping visit with a member of the bishopric before being baptized. This has always been a requirement, but sometimes this important process is overlooked. We are anxious that all converts remain active. The full-time missionaries are encouraged to continue to work and fellowship with their new converts after baptism. Please do this as long as the local leaders feel that help is needed. Our goal is not just a harvest of baptisms; it is a harvest of convert baptisms.

May we all remember that people are important. They are more important than programs. Because we are imperfect, mistakes will be made and feelings occasionally will be hurt. I pray that each of us will stand above petty differences. I pray that we will all be strong enough to lift the weak in the name of Jesus Christ. Amen.

Love,

President Marbury

"Love, teach, convert, baptize—do it now!"

Harvesting And Gleaning

Dear Missionaries,

"But when the fruit is brought forth, immediately he putteth in the sickle, because the harvest is come." (Mark 4:29)

There was a time when the gospel was not to be found upon the earth, at least not in its fullness. During that time the soil was being prepared. The seeds were being sown. Silently and quietly, the fruit was beginning to ripen.

There was a time when the gospel could not be preached freely across the land. Those who preached the gospel were persecuted, ridiculed, and often put to death for their dedication. Joseph Smith is an example. So is his brother Hyrum. So is Jesus Christ.

Here in the United States, we are no longer treated with the violence that once greeted the early missionaries. The soil is prepared. The seeds are sown. The fruit is ripe. Leadership is everywhere. Wards and stakes are well organized. The time of harvest is come.

Repent with all your might, counsels the Savior. Now is your time, your opportunity. You will be missionaries all of your lives, but only for a fraction of your lives will you be called to be full-time harvesters. After the time of the harvest comes the gleaning. To glean is to gather what is left by the reapers. To glean is to search and find the few remaining fruits. Gleaning has its rewards. It is an important and necessary part of the work, but the real rewards come to the harvester.

Our lives are made up of times of sowing, cultivating, harvesting, and gleaning. With respect to the souls of others, now is your time to harvest. You can make it an abundant harvest upon which to add the gleaning of future years, or you can settle for simply the gleaning alone. The choice is yours.

Love,

President Marbury

"The surest way not to fail is to determine to succeed."

—Sheridan

How We Act When No One Knows

Dear Missionaries,

"...Be patient in long-suffering and afflictions, that ye may show forth good examples unto them in me, and I will make an instrument of thee in my hands unto the salvation of many souls." (Alma 17:11)

While attending the seminar for mission presidents in Seattle, Washington, the president of the Oregon Portland mission approached me concerning two of our missionaries here in the Idaho Boise Mission. The missionaries were laboring in LaGrand, Oregon, and were observed by a doctor living in Portland. He was attending a convention for doctors, and was riding in a car with several other doctors, when he observed the missionaries. The doctors, not being members of the Church, saw these two missionaries running down the street and wanted to know what they were doing.

"Why don't we just park the car and watch them a while?" was the reply. They did just that. They parked the car and watched as Elders Duncan and Compton continued to run down the street.

"These two young men are said to represent the true Church. Look how they continue to work hard even when they think no one is watching?"

After several minutes one of the nonmember doctors commented further, "I have never seen a better example of hard work and dedication. I would like to know more about the church that produces this caliber of excellence in its members."

Congratulations Elders Duncan and Compton on your good examples. How we act when we think no one knows who we are is one of the truest tests of character.

God bless you both for your faithfulness.

Love,

President Marbury

"How we act when we think no one knows who we are is one of the truest tests of character."

I Can Do All Things Through Christ

Dear Missionaries,

"I can do all things through Christ which strengtheneth me" (Philippians 4:13). That was Paul's message to the Philippians, and that is my message to you. You can do all things through Christ. As you trust Christ, He will strengthen you to succeed.

Raymond Berry was reaching his goal before most of you were born. His goal in life was to be one of the starting receivers on the Baltimore Colts football team—an ambitious goal for even the best of athletes. For Raymond Berry it was impossible, except Raymond didn't realize it. You see, Raymond was not only sickly but also physically disabled. His weak back required that he be fitted with a back harness. Since one leg was shorter than the other, he wore higher cleats on one shoe to make his stride even. He had severe vision problems requiring strong glasses even to see. He wore contact lenses at every game. But Raymond Berry was determined to use every available minute to perfect himself in his goal of being a starting pass receiver for the Baltimore Colts.

Did he make it? As their star receiver, Raymond Berry led the Baltimore Colts to the National Football League championship in both 1958 and 1959. He became more than a starting receiver for the Baltimore Colts; he became the champion pass receiver for the entire National Football League!

You will accomplish those things you desire enough to persist beyond temporary failures. Christ will strengthen you to succeed as you dedicate to Him your total effort. Give your strength to Christ, and He will give His strength to you.

Love,

President Marbury

"Give your strength to Christ, and He will give His strength to you."

I Can Do More And I Will

Dear Missionaries,

As Jesus was instructing his apostles, he made this comment recorded in Luke 17:10: "So likewise ye, when ye shall have done all those things which are commanded you, say, we are unprofitable servants: we have done that which was our duty to do."

The stress here is on the importance of doing all that is required and more. We cannot magnify our callings by being minimum missionaries. There is a way to do all that the Lord asks and more. Find it. There is a way to develop the faith necessary to draw upon the powers of Heaven. Develop it. There is a way to sanctify ourselves to the point where we have no thoughts, desires, or actions other than those of service to our Heavenly Father. Do it.

You are wonderful missionaries, and my wife and I love you dearly. We want you to have all the blessings of Heaven. Our constant prayer is that you will be pure enough to receive them. You can gain few greater blessings than making for yourselves eternal friends as you prepare them for celestial exaltation through the waters of baptism. We can do much more than we are doing, and we will do it. May the Lord bless each of you.

        Love,

        President Marbury

"I can do more, and I will do it."

Ideas From Missionaries At Zone Conference

Dear Missionaries,

It was good to be with each of you at the zone conferences and to have the privilege of learning from you. Many thoughts were presented during those conferences that I will share here. The ideas came from you. I'm grateful to have been present when they were presented.

Faith is a principle of power in action. Whether we believe we can or can't, we're probably right. Some men's ceilings are other men's floors. We will rise or fall depending on the kind of spirit we have. The spirit of action is the spirit of success. Planning is necessary for real success; however, implementation is the most important part of any plan. No matter how elaborate, no map has ever carried a single person over a single inch of ground. Action is required for success. Act now so that you may say, "It is done," before failure has time to say, "It is too late." Work hard smarter and work smart harder.

President David O. McKay was quoted as saying, "If you want to evaluate yourself, do it with the Holy Ghost present and see yourself as God does." We are called to teach with power in order to gain convert baptisms. Develop vision. Begin with the end in mind. Prepare yourself. Plan to do first things first. Develop the discipline to be strong in the hard moments.

Dear Missionaries

We have set out on our missions of our own free will because we love the Savior and desire to serve Him. He will help us to harvest as we purify ourselves through obedience and hard work. Let us do it now.

Love,

President Marbury

"Evaluate yourself with the Holy Ghost present and see yourself as God does."

—David O. McKay

"If—" By Rudyard Kipling

Dear Missionaries,

At staff meeting the other morning, the following poem by Rudyard Kipling was read for our spiritual thought. I am enclosing it here with the desire that it will uplift you as it did us.

"If—"

If you can keep your head when all about you
Are losing theirs and blaming it on you,
If you can trust yourself when all men doubt you,
But make allowance for their doubting too;
You can wait and not be tired by waiting,
Or, being lied about, don't deal in lies,
Or being hated don't give way to hating,
And yet don't look too good, nor talk too wise:

If you can dream—and not make dreams your master;
If you can think—and not make thoughts your aim,
If you can meet with Triumph and Disaster
And treat those two imposters just the same;
If you can bear to hear the truth you've spoken

Dear Missionaries

Twisted by knaves to make a trap for fools,
Or watch the things you gave your life to, broken,
And stoop and build 'em up with worn-out tools:

If you can make one heap of all your winnings
  And risk it on one turn of pitch-and-toss,
  And lose, and start again at your beginnings,
  And never breathe a word about your loss;
If you can force your heart and nerve and sinew
  To serve your turn long after they are gone,
  And so hold on when there is nothing in you
  Except the Will which says to them: "Hold on!"

If you can talk with crowds and keep your virtue,
Or walk with Kings—nor lose the common touch,
If neither foes nor loving friends can hurt you,
If all men count with you, but none too much;
  If you can fill the unforgiving minute
  With sixty seconds' worth of distance run,
  Yours is the Earth and everything that's in it,
  And—which is more—you'll be a Man, my son!

Love,

President Marbury

"If you can feel the unforgiving minute
With sixty seconds' worth of distance run,
Yours is the Earth and everything that's in it,
And—which is more—you'll be a Man, my son!"

IF YOU WANT A THING BAD ENOUGH

Dear Missionaries,

Several of you have asked for a copy of this poem. Here it is.

If You Want a Thing Bad Enough

If you want a thing bad enough
To go out and fight for it,
Work day and night for it,
Give up your time and your peace and your sleep for it,
If only a desire of it
Makes your arm strong enough
Never to tire of it,
Makes you hold all things tawdry and cheap for it.
If life seems empty and useless without it
And all that you scheme and you dream is about it,
If gladly you sweat for it,
Fret for it,
Plan for it,
Lose all your terror of God and of man for it,
If you'll simply go after the thing that you want,
With all your capacity,

Dear Missionaries

Strength and sagacity,
Faith, hope and confidence, stern pertinacity,
If neither cold, poverty, famished and gaunt,
Nor sickness, nor pain,
Of body and brain,
Can turn you away from the thing that you want,
If dogged and grim you besiege and beset it,
You'll Get It!

—Author unknown

May you all want success enough to get it.

Love,

President Marbury

"Regardless of who you are or what you have been, you can be what you want to be."

I'll Go

Dear Missionaries,

"Let your light so shine before men, that they may see your good works, and glorify your Father which is in heaven." (Matthew 5:16)

I had an uplifting experience in a Church meeting some time ago. The ward was considering a work project that would net a profit of $3,000. The Bishop explained the project and then turned the meeting over to the congregation for discussion. The first comments were negative. "I'm against it!" "I went last time and no one else came!" "Anytime we have one of these projects, the same few do all the work!" The Bishop's eyes seem to sadden as a spirit of negativity clouded the meeting.

Then, as if an angel from Heaven entered the room, Sister Carmichael, a sister missionary who had served in that area, stood and spoke two words: "I'll go!" All contentions ceased as an amazed group listened again to this delightful bundle of enthusiasm. "I'll go!" Frowns transformed into smiles as another replied, "I'll go, too!" "So will my family. We'll all go!" One uncondemning light renewed the spirituality of an entire congregation with only two words.

Messages can be brief and still have decided impact. A few words well-spoken convert far more than a rambling dissertation. The Declaration of Independence contains only 300 words; the Ten

Dear Missionaries

Commandments 297 words; Lincoln's Gettysburg Address 266 words; and the Lord's Prayer only 56 words. A US Government order in the early 1970s setting the price of cabbages contained 26,911 words.

The spirit converts. Righteous action converts. Proper example converts. Enthusiasm converts. Love converts. Do it. My wife and I love you all.

Love,

President Marbury

"All the beautiful sentiments in the world weigh less than a single lovely action."

—James Russell Lowell

IN THE BEGINNING GOD

Dear Missionaries,

Past years are only memories, and a new year begins. It can be our best. Resounding with an eternal message are the first four words we read in the Bible, "In the beginning God..." (Genesis 1:1). Here are some thoughts to help us begin this year with God.

THE POWER OF PRAYER IS REAL—I SHALL USE IT

We talk a lot about daily prayers. This year, let's pray daily. I don't mean the routine prayers of morning, evening, and mealtime. Those are good, but I mean the private, secret prayers that accomplish the miracles of life. The experience of seventeen-year-old Lorraine Wanlund of San Pedro, California is an example.

Lorraine was kidnapped from the front lawn of her home in broad daylight. Immediately her family and community began prayer groups that covered a vast area, like a net slowly tightening about its prey. As Lorraine's abductors entered the freeway, they heard the steady chopping of a low-flying helicopter. Panic-stricken, the kidnappers released her unharmed behind a carpentry shop. Although the police never saw the kidnappers, the noise from their helicopters had saved Lorraine. But as one police officer commented, "Maybe it wasn't helicopter noise—maybe it was angel's wings." Prayer had worked the miracle.

I SHALL ACT—NOT REACT

A young girl stood in church crying. Her runny nose was ruining her dress, and her very presence was causing confusion in general. As several leaders conversed with each other, expressing resentment over anyone who would allow their daughter to cause such disruption, a young teenage girl appeared on the scene. Cleaning the child with a paper towel, she asked the conversing leaders, "Can anyone tell me where to take this little four-year-old to her Sunday school class? She's been crying because she was lost." In a few moments the disturbance was gone and the chapel was quiet. A single loving act of understanding accomplished more than the reactions of almost a dozen well-meaning churchgoers.

I SHALL BE A HAPPY PERSON

William James stated, "The greatest discovery of my generation is that people can alter their lives by altering their attitudes of mind." Abraham Lincoln commented that people are about as happy as they make up their minds to be. This year I am resolved to be a happy person. I invite you to join me.

I SHALL BE A MISSIONARY

The Lord has said in Scripture that the thing of most worth to us is to bring souls to Him (D&C 15:6, 16:6). This year I shall devote more of my time to the important things and less to the trivial. I shall recognize that when a prophet of the Lord counseled each family to bring another soul into the Church this year, this is just as binding on my family as the counsel to do temple work, welfare work, or paying fast offerings. President Kimball told us the steps: (1) prayerfully select a family or families to friendship. (2) be their friends. (3) invite them into your home to be taught by the missionaries. Then President Kimball said, "Do it now!"

The Lord measures our love for Him by how well we keep His commandments. He promises us success and confirms that He is bound when we do what He says. When we refuse, we are left without promise (D&C 82:10). This year I know you will do it. I know you will be the great missionaries that the Lord has called each local member and full-time missionary to be. I love you all and commit to you and to the Lord to do my part also.

Love,

President Marbury

"In the beginning God..."

—Genesis 1:1

It Can Be Done

Dear Missionaries,

During the April 1979 conference, President Spencer W. Kimball said these words,

> The major strides which must be made by the Church will follow upon the major strides to be made by us as individuals. We have paused on some plateaus long enough. Let us resume our journey forward and upward. Let us quietly put an end to our reluctance to reach out to others...Seemingly small efforts in the life of each member could do so much more to move the church forward as never before. Think, brothers and sisters, what would happen if each active family were to bring another family or individual into the church before next April Conference.

IT CAN BE DONE

The conversion and baptism of thousands of souls is the destiny of the Church. If each family in stake presidencies, bishoprics, and relief society presidencies will bring another family of equal size into the church this year, we can all rejoice in the conversion of thousands of souls. Sounds easy, doesn't it? It is. If we desire to follow the prophet enough to actually do what he asked, a miracle will occur. Let's show him and the Savior our love by our actions.

BELIEVE IT

"Jesus said unto him, if thou canst believe, all things are possible to him that believeth" (Mark 9:23). The first step in doing is believing with desire. The more we love our Heavenly Father, the more we desire to help others follow his instructions. We also will believe that the Lord works miracles as we become totally converted. Can't never could. Faint heart never won fair lady. Years ago scientists said that the bumblebee couldn't fly because of the smallness of its wings and the largeness of its body. The bumblebee didn't know that, so it went ahead and flew anyway. The words of Napoleon Hill—"What the mind can conceive and believe it can achieve"—are true. Believe, with desire, and you will attain.

PLAN IT

Now that you believe we are going to baptize thousands, with the Lord's help, as the prophet has directed, plan for it. Schedule regular baptismal services to accomplish your success. Keep a record of the last two times each family has had a prospective convert family taught in their home. If the last time for a particular family was more than six months ago, see if that family is willing to plan for another lovely evening. Regularly express love to new converts and to those who haven't yet received these blessings.

Plan for early priesthood interviews with new converts. Have immediately available a list of needs and ward positions that will effectively utilize the new talent now available. Brainstorm to invent new and more effective ways to share the gospel, both before and after baptism. Remember, although baptism is a commandment and is necessary, the ultimate goal is exaltation in the celestial kingdom.

Dear Missionaries

DO IT

"Where there is nothing to lose by trying and everything to gain if successful, by all means try. Do it now!"—President Spencer W. Kimball

Begin with prayer. Ask Heavenly Father to bless your heart with a love for everyone and a desire to share what you have with others. Converse with the Lord about several nonmembers you know and ask for guidance and the courage to select one family to friendship. Perform an act of friendship for that family this week. Next, be a true friend and invite them into your home to be taught by the missionaries. As they accept baptism through your love and friendship (and, in many instances, courage), you will have an eternal place in their hearts.

Love,

President Marbury

"Where there is nothing to lose by trying and everything to gain if successful, by all means try. Do it now!"

—PRESIDENT SPENCER W. KIMBALL

Jeremy Bentham Syndrome

Dear Missionaries,

"Be ye doers of the word, and not hearers only, deceiving your own selves." (James 1:22)

Ever had the Jeremy Bentham syndrome? Jeremy Bentham, born February 15, 1748, was a philosopher and social theorist. He lived in England, became wealthy, and made a substantial donation to University College London. The donation was made with the stipulation that he would be present at all meetings of the board of directors. When he died, his body was embalmed, dressed in his customary clothes, and preserved in that condition at University College. The board of directors continued to record his attendance at their regular meetings. The secretary would call the roll and then make the following notation beside his name: "Present—but not active!"

What is the status of your activity in the mission field? You are here. You are present. Are you active? What will be the status of your activity in the coming New Year? What will be the status of your spirituality—your attitude? Your attitude will determine your actions, and your actions will determine your success.

Here are some suggestions. Be among the best by working seventy hours in one week. Can you be the best? Can you be a seventy-hour-a-week missionary? Here's how. Leave your apartment by nine o'clock each morning; take only thirty minutes for lunch, one hour for dinner, and leave to proselyte by five thirty in the evening on preparation day. You can gain even more hours by performing service projects on preparation days.

Practice positive performance. Say something positive to everyone you meet. Find something positive in every situation. Act immediately on every positive idea. Expect the best. Verbalize only positive emotions, never negative ones. Remember, you represent the Savior and the Savior is a winner.

Let love govern your every deed, thought and decision. Be a missionary of excellence. May the coming New Year be your best one yet, and may you make every New Year a better one.

Love,

President Marbury

"Practice positive performance."

John Jacob Astor

Dear Missionaries,

As we teach investigators, be conscious of their individual needs. Most of you have heard of John Jacob Astor. What you may not have heard is that this multimillionaire came to America in debt. His success was due to his ability to recognize needs and fulfill them.

When a millinery store whose mortgage Astor held became unable to make its mortgage payments, he foreclosed on it and then went back into business with the same people and with the same capital. The millinery store made bonnets, but had not been able to sell them. Astor went to Central Park, found a bench, sat down, and began watching ladies and their bonnets as they walked by. Having observed and determined what ladies liked and needed in bonnets, he went back to the store and gave instructions concerning precisely what kind of bonnets to make and place in the store windows. That was the beginning of one of the great department stores of New York.

"Search diligently, pray always, and be believing, and all things shall work together for your good, if ye walk uprightly and remember the covenant wherewith ye have covenanted one with another" (D&C 90:24). As you search, you will learn what your investigators need. As you live purely, you will find yourself able to fulfill those needs. Recognize a need and fulfill it. Purify your lives so that you can fulfill the needs effectively.

Love,

President Marbury

"Recognize a need and fulfill it."

Kindness Works

Dear Missionaries,

I read a slogan the other day that simply stated, "Kindness works." This was a change from the old slogan of "Try a little kindness." The new slogan has more merit. Not only is it saying to be kind, but also to work at being kind.

The words "kindness works" first explain how kindness is accomplished. It is accomplished by working. Those who are kind busy themselves with good deeds. They make a conscious effort to do good on purpose.

The words "kindness works" also tell the results of doing good deeds. As we show kindness, we are blessed. As we show kindness to our fellow missionaries, we have more harmony in our companionships, our districts, and our zones. As we show kindness to our investigators, we are blessed with baptisms. As we work at being kind throughout this life, we are blessed with exaltation in the eternal world. May we practice kindness always, I pray in the name of Jesus Christ. Amen.

Love,

President Marbury

"Kindness works."

Let Not Your Hands Be Weak—Work

Dear Missionaries,

Azariah said these words to Asa in the fifteenth chapter of 2 Chronicles

> ...The Lord is with you, while ye be with him; and if you seek him, he will be found of you; but if ye forsake him, he will forsake you....Be strong therefore, and let not your hands be weak: for your work shall be rewarded. (2 Chronicles 15:2, 7)

When Asa heard these words, he took courage and put away the abominable idols and other evils in his land, and made a covenant to seek the Lord God with all his heart and soul. He and his people were rewarded accordingly. If we are to receive the full blessing of our missionary labors, we, too, must put away our abominable idols and covenant with the Lord to serve him. Ninety percent dedication is not good enough for the Lord. He requires one hundred percent effort.

Put away those idols of laziness and partial service and covenant now to serve with all your heart, might, mind, and strength. This is the Lord's work. Covenant with the Lord in the morning that you won't eat lunch until you have taught a discussion, and you will teach. Ask the Lord to guide you to that member who will arrange to have several investigators in their home for a spiritual cottage meeting. Ask in faith, and you will have success. The time is now. The place is your own individual area.

When you're happy, work. When you're sad, work. When you're strong, work. When you're weak, work. Whether you are tired or rested, in the mood or out of the mood, feeling good or feeling bad...work!!!

The prophet Alma said, "I fear exceedingly that the judgments of God will come upon this people, because of their exceeding slothfulness" (Alma 60:14). May we reap rewards rather than judgments through diligent work.

Love,

President Marbury

"Be ye strong, therefore, and let not your hands be weak..."

—2 CHRONICLES 15:7

Lift Up Your Heads

Dear Missionaries,

The other day I ran across a verse, attributed to Susan Coolidge, that I thought you would like. Here it is:

> *Lift up your heads, ye sorrowing ones*
> *And be ye glad at heart.*
> *For Calvary and Easter Day,*
> *Earth's saddest day and gladdest day,*
> *Were just three days apart.*

May your sad days be over and glad days follow you the remainder of your missions and your lives.

Love,

President Marbury

"Be ye glad at heart."

LOVE AND SACRIFICE

Dear Missionaries,

Sometimes, when I am in one of my more melancholy moods, I reflect on our mission here on this earth and whether or not it is being accomplished in the spirit of love taught by the Savior. Sometimes I wonder if we are so caught up in the "bowl of cherries" of life that we haven't time to observe how the "ugly caterpillar" can change into the "beautiful butterfly." Do we search so hard to find the polished diamond that we scramble for every piece of cut glass we see—ignoring the ten-carat gem lying inside its black carbon mask?

LOVE OR JUDGMENT

How much love do we put into our quest to save souls? How much tenderness do we feel for those who, for the present, fail to measure up to our standards of goodness? People change, and they begin to reach their real potential as they are given the opportunity of baptism into the Church of Jesus Christ of Latter-day Saints. The change is usually not immediate. It occurs gradually because of the love shown by some kind member. Converts blossom by experiencing a newfound love for those who are able to love them regardless of faults. Even though they may be unworthy by temple standards, they are accepted for baptism, loved, nurtured, and forgiven as they stumble and fall and are lifted up through the goodness of nonjudgmental saints.

NEW CONVERTS MAKE MANY SACRIFICES

I receive many letters from new converts. The sacrifices to join the Church are real. One teenage convert wrote,

> When the missionary finally brought up the matter of baptism, I was so excited I almost started to cry, because I was so happy. My father agreed to let me join the Church on condition that I quit the drill team. I couldn't drive the car to any Church functions. They wouldn't let me go on dates, or use the car after dark. I still love my parents very much, but I love the LDS Church also. I love the Church and its members, and I know that the gospel is true.

Another wrote,

> After graduation my friend and I went to spend the summer together. She is a very good LDS. I started taking the discussions and was later baptized. When I told Mom, she started crying. That alone almost killed me. My sister said she would disown me, and it totally shocked everything out of my little brother. Dad said if I ever brought my religion into his house or tried to convert any member of my family, I was going out right along with it. Before I left, I really wasn't sure how to say goodbye to my family. I finally just told them I love them and left. I know the Church is true even though it was the hardest decision I've ever made. I know without a doubt it was also the best!

LOVE BRINGS POSITIVE BENEFITS

These words from a kindly new convert show the positive influence of loving members:

Since your letter my husband passed away with cancer. Our faith was put to a supreme test, as well as our love, as the cancer disfigured my husband physically and mentally. My husband wasn't going to be baptized because he felt he wasn't worthy to be a Mormon. He felt since the Mormons are physically fit and a nice-looking people, he didn't measure up. But I prodded him, and we were baptized. We loved each other deeply. Our bishop and his wife were essential in helping with my son when his father died. They cared for him while I watched over my husband in his last hours. The Church has been extremely supportive. Now I've gone off welfare and have only meager Social Security plus a night job. I feel a pride within knowing the Church hasn't a poor, state-supported relative. I plan on continuing to spread the gospel, as it would please my husband.

New converts are the lifeblood of the Church. Their zeal to serve radiates energy, gusto, fervor, and zest. They understand the spirit of urgency called for by President Kimball. Their sincerity awakens the sleeping tenderness that is part of us all, but that we too frequently bury in the scurry of daily activities. We are blessed as they become a part of our lives—and as we become a part of theirs. As we are faithful, these blessings will continue eternally.

Love,

President Marbury

"Love and you shall be loved."

—RALPH WALDO EMERSON

Love, Faith, And Personal Commitment

Dear Missionaries,

Knowing the Savior better, becoming as close to Him as I am to my earthly family, grows more important to me daily. I am convinced that true wisdom does not stand in the wisdom of men, but in the power of God, a power obtained only through spiritual means. I am convinced that the Lord would have us harvest thousands of souls for their sakes and that they, with us, will obtain eternal life. I know that the spiritual power to harvest comes as we are taught from on high, as we converse with Heavenly Father through prayer.

I suggest that prayer power comes through the application of three principles: (1) unfeigned love (2) unwavering faith and (3) personal commitment.

Unfeigned Love

Heavenly Father loves us, His children, and desires us to love each other. Paul said in his letter to the Corinthians, "And now abideth faith, hope, charity, these three; but the greatest of these is charity" (1 Corinthians 13:13).

Unfeigned love is sincere. It is not hypocritical. If we have bad feelings toward others, we gain personal strength by forgiving them and asking them to forgive us. Unfeigned love helps us to hear with our hearts. It prepares us to receive the "heart feelings" through which our Heavenly Father most frequently communicates.

UNWAVERING FAITH

Prayer is power because it adds to our limited abilities a partner with unlimited strength. Yet sometimes, due to our lack of preparation, we fail to use our greatest source of help. The story is told of a young lad whose father asked him move a huge boulder. After repeated attempts, all ending in failure, the boy reported he had done everything he could, but couldn't move it. The father lovingly put his arm around his son and replied, "No son, you haven't done everything. You haven't asked me to help."

James counseled all who seek help from the Lord this way: "But let him ask in faith, nothing wavering. For he that wavereth is like a wave of the sea driven with the wind and tossed" (James 1:6). Heavenly Father loves us and wants to help us, but He will not force us to receive His help. He simply waits, anxious to help those who ask in faith.

PERSONAL COMMITMENT

David O. McKay stated, "Sincere praying implies that when we ask for any virtue or blessing, we should work for the blessing and cultivate the virtue." This means that once we have sought help from Heavenly Father, we have a responsibility to give our total effort to achieving the blessing. The Lord will compensate for our personal weaknesses, but He expects 100 percent of our strength.

In Mosiah 5:5, the people of Zerahemla stated, "And we are willing to enter into a covenant with our God to do his will...". The Lord will bless us as we do the same. We will be blessed as we make and keep covenants with the Lord. As we learn to master ourselves, to overcome carnal desires with spiritual activity, to harvest our own souls and work for the harvest of the souls of others, we will qualify as true representatives of Jesus Christ. We will not just be called to the work. We will be chosen to receive the blessings.

My wife and I love all of you. We pray for you daily and ask that you pray for us. Our heartfelt desire is to increase the already existing spirit of love that pervades this mission. May we all love our neighbors as ourselves and utilize the power of prayer to radiate that love. May it be felt by all, I pray in the name of Jesus Christ. Amen.

Love,

President Marbury

"Faithful prayer and 100 percent effort will reap the harvest."

Love Is The Key To Life

Dear Missionaries,

"Be kindly affectioned one to another, with brotherly love; in honor preferring one another." (Romans 12:10)

Love is the key to life, success, and happiness. The gospel is a gospel of love. Our message is a message of love. Christ's example was an example of love. Without love, life would simply cease to exist.

There is documented evidence that the absence of love will destroy an individual emotionally as well as physically. The thirteenth-century experiment of Frederick II offers a vivid example. Seeking to learn what language children would speak if they never heard the spoken word, he placed fifty infants under the care of foster parents. The foster parents could bathe and feed the infants but were forbidden to caress or talk to them. The experiment failed. Not because the foster parents failed to carry out the conditions of the experiment precisely—they did. It failed because all fifty infants died. Deprived of love, they simply quit living and died.

Deprived of love, society will die. Void of understanding for one another, companionships will suffer. Without a natural affection for those whom we teach, our message will cease to bear fruit. More important than what we say is the feeling we convey as we say it. When spirit speaks with spirit, miracles happen.

Conversion is the natural result. The spirit speaks always in an atmosphere of love. May you live so you will always be worthy of the spirit, I pray in the name of Jesus Christ. Amen.

Love,

President Marbury

"One may be better than his reputation, but never better than his principles."

—Nicholas V. de Latena

LOVE ONE ANOTHER

Dear Missionaries,

Henry D. Taylor once told of a young Persian student in Munich, Germany. The young man was bitter about the selfishness and materialism filling the world. When two Latter-day Saint missionaries came to his door, he invited them in with the statement, "Don't tell me about your God or your religion. Tell me what you do for one another."

After a short pause, one of the missionaries replied, "We love one another." This simple utterance so filled the soul of this young Persian student that he was baptized shortly thereafter.

Christ said, "If ye love me, keep my commandments" (John 14:15). As we begin a new year, we begin again to fulfill the covenants we made with the Lord. We each covenanted that we would serve Him with all our heart, might, mind, and strength. We agreed to serve wherever we were called—city or county, in a car or on a bike, as a zone leader or a junior companion. We knew trials would come. We knew many would be called to serve over us who have faults and weaknesses just as we have. We covenanted to sustain these leaders, to refrain from criticizing them in any way, and to build them up in the eyes of our fellow missionaries. We covenanted never to seek glory or honor or position for ourselves. We understood that the purpose of our mission is to serve others and not ourselves. We understood that the greatest of all is the servant of all. In simple language, we covenanted to love one another.

My wife and I love you all and desire to serve you. Our prime concern is your eternal welfare. Along with you, we also love those wonderful people who are yet to accept the gospel. This year my family and I renew our covenants to serve the Lord with exactness. We renew our covenants to work harder, smarter, and with greater love. We encourage you to do likewise.

Love,

President Marbury

"Love one another."

Love Your Calling

Dear Missionaries,

My wife and I are thrilled to be associated with the number one mission in the Church. Your enthusiasm in serving our Heavenly Father is uplifting to me and my family. We all are committing ourselves to remain pure and upright before the Lord. Realizing that purity comes before all else, will you make commitments to do the following?

1. **Know Your Calling**. All discussions and scriptures should be passed off within two or three months, and then a proficiency level of 75 percent perfect should be maintained throughout our mission. I ask that you also memorize D&C 11:21.
2. **Love Your Calling**. Love your Heavenly Father and Jesus Christ. Love your companion. Love your investigators. Love your work. "And now abideth faith, hope, charity, these three; but the greatest of these is charity" (I Corinthians 13:13).
3. **Believe Your Calling**. If you believe you can't do it, you can't. If you believe you can do it, and work for it, you can. It can be done!
4. **Magnify Your Calling**. We may have a perfect knowledge, love, and belief, but without works, these will bring no

rewards. Belief only places us on a level with the devil, who also believes and trembles (James 2:19–20). To magnify our calling we must be doers (James 1:22).

Remember the instruction from the Lord on how to obtain wisdom from Him. Study it out in your mind. Plan for success and then present that plan to the Lord for His approval (D&C 9:7–8). May the Lord bless you as you serve Him.

Love,

President Marbury

"Know, love, believe, and magnify your calling."

Make A Zion Mission

Dear Missionaries,

The story is told of a group of people waiting at a toll bridge to win the $500 that would be given to the one millionth car to cross the bridge. As a driver approached, he saw the sign requiring payment of one dollar to cross. Refusing to pay, he turned around and went the other way. The next car paid and received the reward.

During the past zone conferences, all have expressed the desire to establish a Zion Mission. To gain the reward, we must pay the price. Zion begins with each companionship. As has been said many times, if you think you have a lemon for a companion, make lemonade out of him or her.

As we establish Zion, we will baptize many souls for the Lord. You are celestial missionaries. You can do it. "And the Lord called his people Zion because they were of one heart and one mind, and dwelt in righteousness; and there was no poor among them" (Moses 7:18).

Love,

President Marbury

"When we conclude to make a Zion, we will make it, and this work commences in the heart of each person."

—Brigham Young

MAKE CHRIST THE CENTER OF YOUR LIFE

Dear Missionaries,

I was listening to a tape recently by Stephen R. Covey entitled *Make Christ the Center of Your Life*. In it he listed six basic habits of a truly effective person. I was so impressed with his message that I am listing them here for your benefit:

1. **Spiritually create each day in your mind before living it**. There are no physical victories before there are first mental or spiritual victories. See yourself as the Lord sees you, as a child of God. You have unlimited potential when you know who you truly are.
2. **Do first things first**. Prioritize, schedule, discipline.
3. **Take responsibility for your own life**. Don't blame others for your problems. You always have the freedom to choose your response in every situation. Be a producer, not a consumer. Be a light, not a judge. Be a model, not a critic.
4. **Think win-win**. Most of us are brought up to think, "I win, you lose," or, "I lose, you win." The mature person will discuss every challenge to determine a solution that will please everyone. "Everybody wins" requires both courage and consideration—courage for you to win and consideration for the other person to win as well.

5. **Seek first to understand before seeking to be understood.** How often do we listen in order to reply rather than to understand? Seek first to understand.
6. **Put Christ at the center of your life**. Build a foundation on the Savior of the world with regard to security, wisdom, direction, and power. As you do this, your life will be in proper balance.

God bless you to be truly effective as you apply the six principles.

Love,

President Marbury

"Be a model not a critic."

Make Your Performance Match Your Potential

Dear Missionaries,

Last week at zone conferences we were blessed to receive much good advice from one of the Lord's chosen servants, Elder Derek A. Cuthbert. As he counseled us to "make our performance match our potential," he continued by advising us to ask ourselves ten questions designed to help us measure our performance:

1. How will my companion remember me? How do I want him or her to remember me?
2. How will my investigators remember me? How do I want them to remember me?
3. Am I giving 100 percent effort?
4. Am I petitioning the Lord or just saying my prayers?
5. Have I developed a true love of Jesus Christ?
6. Do I have an eye single to the Lord's work?
7. Do I look for good in everyone?
8. Do I follow the Lord's guideline on how to be a disciple (*The Missionary Handbook*)?
9. Do I picture them in white?
10. Do I work with the urgency that Present Kimball says I should?

Elder Cuthbert went on to teach us that the best way to show love to our neighbors is to baptize them. We are called to be diligent in serving the Lord. The purpose of our activity is to get results. Although both have proper reasons, there is a significant difference between the missionary who comes on his mission so he can grow and progress and the missionary who comes on his mission to serve, baptize, and show gratitude to the Savior.

Elder Cuthbert explained that obstacles are what we see when we take our eyes off our goals. As Heber J. Grant taught, "No obstacles are insurmountable when God commands and we obey." You are great, and you can be greater. Do you have the attitude "I will not be average"?

President Kimball was quoted frequently about his concern for missionary work and his prayers asking the Lord to bless each missionary with thousands of baptisms:

A mission is a foundation for a lifetime of service and an eternal life of service. There is urgency in our program. We are directed and commanded to convert the world. Evangelistic harvest is always urgent. Let us go forward by leaps and bounds.

Love,

President Marbury

"Are you a leaping and bounding missionary?"

Making Friends

Dear Missionaries,

One of our main purposes in life is to be a friend and to make friends. Perhaps this poem by an unknown author will be motivating for you.

Making Friends

If nobody smiled and nobody cheered
And nobody helped us along,
If every man just looked at himself
And good things all went to the strong.

If nobody cared just a little for you
And nobody thought about me
And we all stood alone in the battle of life,
What a dreary old world it would be.

Life's sweet just because of the friends we have made,
And the things in common we share.
We want to live on, not because of ourselves
But because of the people who care.

Dear Missionaries

It's giving and doing for somebody else,
On that all life's splendor depends.
And the joy of the world when you've summed it all up
Is found in the making of friends.

Life itself can't give you joy
Unless you really will it.
Life just gives you time and space.
It's up to you to fill it.

Love,

President Marbury

"Life just gives you time and space.
It's up to you to fill it."

Many Great Leaders Were Once Called Failures

Dear Missionaries,

The month of April is the month of Christ's birthday. This year April is also the month of Easter. I'm grateful for each of you. Thanks for your love and dedication. I'm grateful that all of you are staying faithful to your callings to serve with all your heart, might, mind, and strength. I'm grateful that you have remained strong in the hard moments.

Isn't it interesting how faith and persistence triumph in the end? Many of the great leaders of the world were first considered failures. Winston Churchill flunked the qualifying exams for Sandhurst Military Institution for three consecutive years, despite special tutoring. Thomas Edison was once at the bottom of his class. One teacher called Henry Ford "a student who showed no promise." Albert Einstein flunked math and was called mentally slow. Of Jesus Christ they said, "Can any good thing come out of Nazareth?" (John 1:46).

Dear Missionaries

No one fails until they fail to persist. You shall all succeed. God bless you for your faithfulness.

Love,

President Marbury

"No one fails until they fail to persist."

THE MIRACLE OF FAITHFULNESS

Dear Missionaries,

Early in my mission I had a most uplifting experience that I would like to share. Through the faithfulness of the parents of one of our missionaries, a miracle took place.

The father, several years ago, developed a very rare disease called myasthenia gravis. This is a muscular disease that is almost always fatal. The father couldn't talk, chew food, or swallow. He could not lift his arms over his head. His face was paralyzed to such an extent that even smiling was impossible. He had no control over his neck muscles and, consequently, was required to wear a neck brace. He felt numb over his entire body.

While in this condition, his bishop visited his home and called him to the position of assistant ward clerk. The father explained that this was impossible. He couldn't even lift his arms, much less write. The father's mind then flashed back to his patriarchal blessing, which promised him blessings, both spiritually and physically, if he would be faithful to his Church callings. Relying on pure faith, he accepted the call. Through the power of the priesthood, the bishop promised the father that he would recover as he remained faithful.

I talked to that father later, during his son's mission. He is well, active, and happy. He is magnifying his calling as assistant ward clerk. He has one thriving business and is starting a second. His family is so excited over the faithfulness of their missionary son, he told me, that they felt added strength as a family. Even the nonmembers in their family are gaining a testimony through the faithfulness of their missionary son.

The Lord performs miracles as we are faithful. May we always be so.

Love,

President Marbury

"...All things are possible to him that believeth."

—Mark 9:23

MISSIONARIES ARE TEACHERS

Dear Missionaries,

"...The Lord will remember the prayers of the righteous." (Mormon 5:21)

The Lord keeps his promises and will remember and answer our prayers when we are righteous. We are here for the purpose of serving the Lord. The people of this mission need the message we have been called to deliver. We have the responsibility of being righteous enough to carry with us the spirit of conversion.

Stephen R. Covey writes of the differences between missionaries who are teachers and those who are salesmen. The teacher is motivated by a genuine regard and love of others, the salesmen by gain or recognition. The teacher works for convert baptisms, which will result in blessing the lives of others; the salesman simply wants to put them in the water. The teacher is honorable to the core. The teacher knows that the means and the end are inseparable. The good teacher demonstrates, motivates, and inspires. The eternal happiness and well-being of those whom he teaches are his prime concern.

Let no one rationalize that they may reach fewer people because they teach rather than sell. While the salesman may exist on a small quantity of sales, we are called to teach, convert, and baptize all who are honest in heart. We must miss no one. Honorable sales techniques are both acceptable and desirable when the goal is to teach and bless the lives of those with whom we come in contact. We must pray daily for the harvest and live righteously enough to have our prayers answered.

I encourage you to continue to work for a Zion companionship and Zion mission. You have been called to harvest. As you follow the Lord's plan, you will do so.

Love,

President Marbury

"Zion is as Zion does."

My Missionary Commitment— Don't Quit

Dear Missionaries,

There comes a time in the lives of all people when they must seal with their actions their testimony of those principles in which they profess to believe. There comes a time in the lives of all people when they must sacrifice to maintain those blessings they hold most sacred. There comes a time in the lives of all people when they must cease asking, "Why me?," and begin asking, "Why not me?". That time is now.

My Missionary Commitment

We have a divine commission to present the gospel to all the world. We begin in our own family. May I suggest that each family hold a family council and evaluate last year's missionary efforts? They could then make a family missionary commitment for the coming year. This commitment could include setting specific dates during the year when they will invite the full-time missionaries to teach the gospel to one of their nonmember friends or families. It could specify a number of copies of the Book of Mormon that they will give to others who may not have read the book. It could include the commitment to pray daily so that the Lord will lead them to someone with whom they may share the gospel. It could also include other missionary ideas of specific actions that can be taken by the family. These family commitments should be written down and followed up with during family home evenings. One member of the family could be asked to be the family missionary chairperson, and that person could take reports of what each family member is doing to meet his or her missionary commitment. The report should be taken and recorded on a regular basis—each month or perhaps every three months.

DO IT

The family missionary commitment process is a simple one, certain to bring improved results. As our leaders have told us, "As an activity is measured, it increases. As it is measured and reported, it increases at an increasing rate." The principle here is simply to commit every family to become anxiously engaged in missionary work and to report their progress.

You have heard it said often, "All that is necessary for the triumph of evil is for good men to do nothing." Things may not always proceed smoothly, but we must always persist. May we all immediately put our hands to the plow, and in so doing, never quit. This poem by an anonymous author says it well.

Don't Quit

When things go wrong, as they sometimes will,
When the road you're trudging seems all up hill,
When the funds are low and the debts are high,
And you want to smile, but you have to sigh,
When care is pressing you down a bit,
Rest if you must—but don't you quit.

Life is queer with its twists and turns,
As every one of us sometimes learns,

My Missionary Commitment—Don't Quit

And many a failure turns about
When he might have won had he stuck it out.
Don't give up, though the pace seems slow—
You might succeed with another blow.

Often the goal is nearer than
It seems to a faint and faltering man.
Often the struggler has given up
When he might have captured the victor's cup
And he learned too late, when the night slipped down,
How close he was to the golden crown.

Success is failure turned inside out—
The silver tint of the clouds of doubt—
And you never can tell how close you are,
It may be near when it seems afar.
So stick to the fight when you're hardest hit—
It's when things seem worst that you mustn't quit.
—Anonymous

May the Lord bless you to seek diligently after others to love into His kingdom—and never to quit.

Love,

President Marbury

"When care is pressing you down a bit,
Rest if you must—but don't you quit."

Neglect Not The Gift That Is In Thee

Dear Missionaries,

"Neglect not the gift that is in thee" (I Timothy 4:14). These words of Paul to Timothy apply as well to you missionaries. You are called of God, by a prophet, to teach and baptize. You have authority to represent the Lord, and you have power from Heaven in accordance with your own personal purity. Are you living worthily enough to call down the powers of Heaven, and are you using the power and the gift that are in you?

Two gifts are of major significance in missionary work—your testimony and your power and authority to act for Christ.

In your testimony lies a great power to convert. Testify always of your knowledge of the truth. Don't be afraid or forget to testify that baptism will open the gate to eternal happiness. The converting power of your testimony lies dormant until used. Your testimony is a great gift from God. Neglect not this gift.

Christ taught us to do all things in His name. You have His power and His authority. Use them. Testify in the name of Jesus Christ that you are teaching truth. As you live purely and cleanly, call upon the powers of Heaven that you may promise blessings in the name of Jesus Christ. Commit with power by testifying in the name of Jesus Christ that the Savior has sent you to your investigators' home to help them repent of their sins and receive the blessings of baptism into the Kingdom of God.

You have the authority. Your purity will give you the power. Some of you will even perform miracles. The destiny of your mission is to baptize thousands. It can be done, I testify to you in the name of Jesus Christ. Amen.

Love,

President Marbury

"Neglect not the gift that is in thee."

—I Timothy 4:14

NEHEMIAH AND THE WALL

Dear Missionaries,

"And I sent messengers unto them, saying, I am doing a great work, so that I cannot come down: why should the work cease, whilst I leave it, and come down to you?" (Nehemiah 6:3)

Nehemiah loved Jerusalem, and the wall protecting it from its enemies was broken down. He asked the king for permission to go and repair the wall. Permission was granted, a prayer was offered, and Nehemiah set about his task.

Enemies of Jerusalem—Sanballat, Tobiah, and Geshem—opposed the work. They laughed—and Nehemiah worked on. Nehemiah and his people were mocked and ridiculed. Their enemies taunted, "...Even that which they build, if a fox go up, he shall even break down their stone wall." (Nehemiah 4:3) But Nehemiah and his people "had a mind to work," and they worked without ceasing.

Soon the wall was built; only the gate lacked completion. Sanballat, Tobiah, and Geshem made one last try. "Come, let us meet together in one of the villages," they said to Nehemiah. The invitation was clever, a subtle way to distract Nehemiah from the work.

Nehemiah's answer was inspired: "I am doing a great work, so that I cannot come down: why should the work cease, whilst I leave it, and come down to you?" Four times the invitation came. Four times it was refused. Fifty-two days later the wall was finished, and all that saw it knew that it was the work of God.

You are doing a great work. The forces of evil will combine to stop you. They will laugh, scorn, despise, mock, and ridicule. They will try to divert you from the work in seemingly innocent ways. Whatever the tactics of the adversary, remember Nehemiah—and work—and all that see it will know it is the work of God.

Love,

President Marbury

"Work—and you will succeed—and all that see it will know it is the work of God."

NIGHT BEFORE CHRISTMAS, WITH APOLOGIES

Dear Missionaries,

I found a poem I wrote when I was twelve, concerning the night before Christmas. I thought you might like it. Here it is.

The Night before Christmas, With Apologies to Clement Clark Moore

'Twas the night before Christmas when all through the house
All was stirring, including the mouse.
I looked at the stockings to be sure to find
The biggest one there, not yours, but mine.
The children all went to bed very quick,
But I stayed up waiting for Old Saint Nick.
When all of a sudden I saw in the sky
Old Saint Nicholas riding by.
Old Saint Nicholas riding behind
The reindeer, there were not eight, but nine.
The leader not Dasher, not Dancer, not Prancer or Vixen,
Not Comet, not Cupid, not Donder or Blitzen,

Night Before Christmas, With Apologies

But Rudolph the red-nosed reindeer ahead
Guiding old Santa Claus's sled.
He stopped at my house along the way,
And went down the chimney without the sleigh.
A watch for daddy, for mother some gloves,
For brother a cap and a gun to shoot doves.
But in my stocking he left behind
A big lump of coal—all mine!
     —Ritchey M. Marbury III

May you get more than a big lump of coal in your Christmas stocking this year. May you have a great harvest.

Love,

President Marbury

"A harvest of convert baptisms is better than a big lump of coal."

No One Goes Far Looking Into the Rearview Mirror

Dear Missionaries,

"Watch therefore, that ye may be ready. Even so. Amen" (D&C 50:46). This verse certainly applies to me. It was three thirty yesterday afternoon as Elder Waldie and I made our way down Franklin Street in Boise, Idaho. We were riding in my three-week-old blue Chevy Citation as we stopped for a red light. A Chevy truck stopped just ahead of us. The light changed to green, and the truck moved ahead slowly in a right turn. I followed, continuing straight down Franklin.

Then it happened. A young boy dashed in front of the truck. The driver put on the brakes. The truck stopped several yards in front of the boy. In the meantime, seeing that the light had changed and that the truck ahead was moving forward, I had glanced in the rearview mirror for about one second. That was the wrong second!

"Look out!" warned Elder Waldie, but it was too late. I quickly applied the brakes. Not soon enough. One embarrassing thud later I was guilty of being responsible for one of those "preventable" accidents I had been lecturing the office staff about. When I returned my car to the office to make out the accident report and arrange for repairs, I asked Elder Tatham for the keys to another

No One Goes Far Looking Into The Rearview Mirror

car. He handed me the keys to a white Chevy Nova. I took them and left the office to drive home. As I started to drive out of the parking lot, I noticed a small handwritten note on the glove compartment. Surely the office staff didn't have time to place it there before I took the car. The note read, "No one goes far just looking into the rearview mirror!"

We can avoid costly and embarrassing situations most of the time by simply being watchful, by being alert, and by paying attention to what we're doing. How often do we find ourselves late to appointments or even missing some appointments completely? Do we sometimes find ourselves saying the wrong thing and getting exactly the results we knew we would but wished we wouldn't? How alert are we to the little virtues that bring big victories? How careful are we to avoid the preventable mistakes that result in costly consequences? I have surely learned my lesson.

Love,

President Marbury

"No one goes far just looking into the rearview mirror!"

Opportunity

Dear Missionaries,

The strong make opportunities out of trials. The weak make trials out of opportunities. The courageous turn disaster into victory. The coward turns victory into disaster. This poem by Edward R. Sill illustrates how one man's defeat is another man's opportunity.

Opportunity

This I beheld, or dreamed it in a dream:—
There spread a cloud of dust along a plain;
And underneath the cloud, or in it, raged
A furious battle, and men yelled, and swords
Shocked upon swords and shields. A prince's banner
Wavered, then staggered backward, hemmed by foes.
A craven hung along the battle's edge,
And thought, "Had I a sword of keener steel—
That blue blade that the king's son bears—but this
Blunt thing—!" he snapped and flung it from his hand,
And lowering crept away and left the field.
Then came the king's son, wounded, sore bestead,

Opportunity

And weaponless, and saw the broken sword,
Hilt buried in the dry and trodden sand,
And ran and snatched it, and with battle-shout
Lifted afresh he hewed his enemy down,
And saved a great cause that heroic day.
—Edward R Sill

God bless you to make every event in your life an opportunity.

Love,

President Marbury

"The strong make opportunities out of trials. The weak make trials out of opportunities."

Opportunity Of A Lifetime And A Lifetime Of Opportunity

Dear Missionaries,

Thanks for being the wonderful missionaries you are. The Lord has raised you up to excel here at this time, and you are doing it. You are today where your thoughts and actions have brought you. Tomorrow you will be where your thoughts and actions take you. I commend to you pure thoughts, thoughts of thankfulness in service, and Christlike action.

Your calling to give full-time service to the Lord is the opportunity of a lifetime; however, it will last only for the lifetime of the opportunity. Serve well in this time of opportunity. Serve that you may bring success to others, and success will be your constant companion.

December is the month in which we celebrate the birth of the Savior. His gift to us was His life, atonement, death, and resurrection. Our gift to Him can be souls who are converted to the true gospel of love, service, and sacrifice. Baptism into His Kingdom is evidence of such conversion. May we set a new record of committed souls to bring this world closer to Christ.

May this be our gift to Him, I pray in the name of Jesus Christ. Amen.

>Love,

>President Marbury

"...And they shall call his name Emmanuel, which being interpreted is, God with us."

—Matthew 1:23

Our Mission—Represent The Savior

Dear Missionaries,

Sometimes, when it seems that nothing is going right, I like to take extra time to reflect on the life and teachings of Jesus. Jesus was the most perfect man who ever lived. He was the most loving man who ever lived. He probably was also the most persecuted man who ever lived. Despite all this, He never complained about those things that happened to Him. After all, His mission was to serve—and save—mankind.

Our mission is to represent the Savior. We are called to act as He would act were He in our place. We have taken a covenant to serve Him with all our hearts, might, minds, and strength. He judges our love for Him by how diligently we do those things we are sent to do. Do we sincerely seek to serve Him ahead of ourselves? Can we truly say in our hearts that we are more interested in service than in position? When our hearts are pricked, do we become defensive and begin criticizing others? Are we making excuses for not working to our maximum capacity? What would the Savior do in our situation?

Today is the day to repent. None of us is perfect, but even that isn't an acceptable excuse. Let us forget ourselves in service to the Savior—now. Let us see improvement in everything we do. Let us create ideas to enrich others. Let us smile more. A smile enriches those who receive it, without impoverishing the one who gives it. Let us become kind by thinking kind thoughts.

Let us baptize. The goal of missionary work is convert baptisms. Never forget that goal. Entrance into the celestial kingdom will come only after baptism. Love Jesus Christ enough to work every minute. The pain and suffering that Christ endured was to make possible baptism for the remission of sins. Let us see that He did not suffer in vain for any person in our area of service.

Love,

President Marbury

"Win souls, not arguments."

Pay The Price

Dear Missionaries,

Recently I heard a tape by Earl Nightingale in which he referred to law of physics stating that for every action there must be an equal and opposite reaction. He then went on to explain that, in plain language, this law means that in order to gain success in any endeavor, we must be willing to pay the price.

We have dedicated ourselves to developing a Zion Mission. The blessings for such are numerous, but there is a price. The price is hard work, love, patience, and understanding.

In the business community, we often obtain the product first and pay later. However, no one can buy on credit in the Lord's Kingdom. We pay the price first, and then the Lord blesses us. We cannot lose our tempers, blame our companions for our problems, or act primarily for ourselves and gain the blessings of a Zion Mission. We cannot say that we will keep the rules on the condition that our companions act as we desire. That's trying to buy the Lord's blessings on credit. It won't work.

Pay The Price

There is a price for a Zion Mission. Pay it, and your investment will multiply into eternal happiness and the harvest.

Love,

President Marbury

"No one can buy on credit in the Lord's Kingdom."

Perform One Successful Act Many Times

Dear Missionaries,

"When we think of our alternatives in conversion rates as being hasty and numerous baptisms on the one hand, and slow, snail-like growth of the Church on the other hand, we are displaying too little faith in the Lord and even in ourselves. These are not our only choices...we can baptize more people, and we can do it in a very solid and stable way."—Spencer W Kimball

The Lord's counsel is clear. We lead as we develop the desire to serve, the knowledge to act, and the experience to succeed.

DESIRE TO SERVE

What can I do to increase my service to Jesus Christ? Christlike service begins with unselfish desire. The story is told of a man named Glen Barney, who was offered a lucrative position that would provide financial security for many years. His four-year-old son, Jerry, overheard Glen telling his wife that he would have to refuse the job since it would cause him to be out of town often during his first year. Jerry's legs were partially paralyzed due to a crippling disease. Glen told his wife that when Jerry was well enough to walk around the house, he would take the job.

Nearly an hour later, Jerry was seen falling tiredly through the front door. His lips were bleeding. His clothes were torn, but his face radiated with the smile of personal achievement. "I fell a lot, daddy, and I tore some of the rosebushes when I fell in them," explained Jerry. "But," he said proudly, "I made it. I walked around the entire house. Now you can take that job!" An overwhelmingly unselfish desire to serve—that's the first step.

KNOWLEDGE TO ACT

Service is commendable. Leadership in service is greatness. This requires knowledge. The most effective approach used in our mission thus far is for local members and leaders to simply ask one or more nonmembers each week, "Do you like to read?" This is an approach taught by Elder Hartman Rector of the Presidency of the Seventy.

Regardless of the answer, follow up with this second question, "If I send you a book containing the actual account of the visit of Jesus Christ to America, will you read it?" Most will say, "Yes. Thank you." Next have the person write his or her name, address, and telephone number on a card or piece of paper and give it to you to have delivered with their book.

You now have the opportunity to personalize a copy of the Book of Mormon with your testimony and a picture of your family. Sometimes you will want to deliver this personally. As friendship and interest develops, you will want to invite the missionaries to teach this family in your home. Other personalized copies of the Book of Mormon will most effectively be delivered by the missionaries. The card with the person's name written in that person's own handwriting will be an effective introduction for the missionaries as they give the most accurate written account of Christ's visit to America. The more the person learns about the Savior, Jesus Christ, the better his or her life will be now and throughout eternity.

EXPERIENCE TO SUCCEED

Know-how is gained from experience. Self-confidence comes from making a habit of success. Successful habits come from performing one successful act many times. "Now ye may suppose that this is foolishness in me; but behold I say unto you, that by small and simple things are great things brought to pass; and small means in many instances doth confound the wise" (Alma 37:6). It isn't necessary to attempt big things to lead in service. Learn through experience to do one thing well and do it many times. Success comes to the steady—to those who persist. May you develop one successful habit to perform many times, I pray in the name of Jesus Christ. Amen.

Love,

President Marbury

"Successful habits come from performing one successful act many times."

Persistence

Dear Missionaries,

In thinking of the many virtues that bring success, I believe one of the most important is persistence. Ability is desirable, but ability comes primarily through stick-ability. The victor is that unremitting individual who tries and fails, but never fails to try again.

Many of the men and women we think of as the most successful in life were at first the most unsuccessful. They experienced the most consistent failures. Abraham Lincoln failed in his business in 1831 and in 1833. He suffered a nervous breakdown in 1836 and lost elections in 1832, 1838, 1840, 1848, 1855, 1856, and 1858. He was elected president of the United States in 1860. Thomas Edison experienced more than ten thousand failures while working to develop the incandescent lamp. Just think—ten thousand failures before one success.

Henry J. Kaiser reported that he failed in 75 percent of the things he tried. What were his successes? Among others he built 1500 merchant ships during World War II and produced more than one million tons of steel and twenty million pounds of magnesium. He was the world's largest producer of cement and the world's third-largest producer of aluminum. The San Francisco–Oakland Bridge as well as the Grand Coulee and Hoover Dams were all constructed with his assistance.

Dear Missionaries

Success is more a journey than a destination. The rewards go to those who persist after all others quit. How do you choose?

Love,

President Marbury

"I shall always succeed, for I shall always persist."

Pick Up Your Sox

Dear Missionaries,

As we strive to be pure in all things, may we not only keep our thoughts clean but also our living conditions so that our apartments may uplift us as we study and pray there. My wife, Sister Fonda Marbury, wrote a poem that can serve as a reminder to us all of how we should keep clean living conditions. I am reproducing it for you here.

Pick Up Your Sox

Pick up your socks and make your bed.
Then set your table—so bountifully spread.
Wash your dishes all shiny and bright—
Mold discourages appetite.
Wash yourself all clean and spiffy—
A shower a day takes only a jiffy.
At a DA please be polite—
Stay only one hour and not all night.
Use your very best manners, you strong and able—
And get those elbows off the table.
Every Monday, without fail,

Dear Missionaries

Clean your floors with mop and pail.
Wash your car, wash your clothes,
Change your sheets, goodness knows!
Clean the bathroom, and the doors,
Write your letters, do your chores.
Always remember who you are—
You may be someone's shining star.
If you're always faithful and true,
Your Heavenly Father will be proud of you.

May the Lord bless you. I love you all.

                    Love,

                    President Marbury

"What was yesterday's impossible is today's outer limit and tomorrow's commonplace."

Plan Your Work

Dear Missionaries,

"Oh how great the plan of our God!" (2 Nephi 9:13). We bear testimony often that God's plans will surely be accomplished. That's true. How often, however, do we realize the example He set by actually planning in the first place? It has truly been stated that when you fail to plan, you plan to fail. Please allow me, here, to present six steps to help you plan more effectively.

1. PRAY

When we plan, we want to be sure our plans are in harmony with those of the Savior. Perhaps too often we rely on our own wisdom when greater wisdom is available from the source of all wisdom. All planning should begin by seeking guidance from the spirit.

2. SET SPECIFIC GOALS

If you were handed a roadmap and told to "go there!" but not told where "there" was, your chances of arriving at the proper destination would be slight. Your chances of real success in time or eternity are just as slight unless you determine specifically where you desire to go. To resolve "I will love two families into the

Church this year," will prove substantially more successful than to make the general statement "I will be a member missionary this year." Remember, a magnifying glass can start a fire only when it is used to focus the sun's rays on a specific point. If we keep moving the magnifying glass, we'll get no flame.

3. STUDY EXISTING CONDITIONS

Just as we can't get "there" if we don't know where "there" is, we also will have difficulty getting "there" unless we know where we are starting from. Who of our friends most closely live the commandments and allow their lives to be governed by the spirit of love? What gospel principles will bring the greatest help to our friends at this time? What church meetings or programs will help or interest our friends? What conditions exist that will help us reach our goals?

4. LIST AND ANALYZE COURSES OF ACTION

What can be done with what exists? Brainstorm. List every idea you can think of without judging its value. Then evaluate the ideas, eliminating those of little or no value. Rate the remaining ideas in order of their value in accomplishing your desired goal.

5. PLAN YOUR WORK

Plan to do the most important things first. Never let those things that matter least get in the way of those things that matter most. When planning, always consider plans for long- and short-range goals. Think big. Make big plans, plans large enough to have the magic to stir the soul. Remember, if you reach for the stars, you won't end up with a bucket of mud.

6. WORK YOUR PLAN

The price of success is lower than the price of failure. You planned for success. Now work and achieve it. While serving the

Savior, put aside things extraneous to the work. Let your work always reflect God's love for His children.

Energy can be used to accomplish good or evil. Just working isn't enough. Working our plan, conceived through the Spirit of the Lord, is necessary for righteous accomplishment. You are what you plan and work to become. A steel bar may be fashioned into doorstops, horseshoes, or main springs for precision watches. Depending on its use, its value will vary from five dollars to a quarter of a million dollars. Your value in time and eternity will depend on how you plan and use your life. Use it well. As you consecrate your life toward saving the souls of others, you will never have to worry about saving your own.

Love,

President Marbury

"You are what you plan and work to become."

Power Through Purity

Dear Missionaries,

I feel a strong need to stress the importance of total purity. You are wonderful missionaries and on the brink of greatness. You are 90 percent there. Satan knows this and is employing all his powers to stop you. You have the power to prevent him, but you have to use it.

There is a great difference between the authority of the priesthood and the power of the priesthood. The authority was given to you when you came on a mission. Power comes only through obedience and sacrifice. You may be blessed with baptisms for a short period while violating mission guidelines. The Lord will allow no one to stop His work. The real blessings, however, come only when you're pure enough to draw on the powers of Heaven. Both baptisms and inner peace are the blessings of a pure mission.

The power to draw on the resources of heaven is given to both elder and sister missionaries. The elders exercise this power through their priesthood office, the sisters through fervent prayer. Purity, total purity with faith, is necessary for a complete manifestation of the power of God through you.

Elder David W. Patten was a missionary in Tennessee when he met a woman who was sick and had been bedridden for one year. When the woman stated that she believed in Jesus Christ,

Elder Patten took her by the hand and said, "In the name of Jesus Christ, arise!" She did. He blessed her, rebuked her disease, and promised her she would bear children, even though she had been childless for the seven years of her marriage.

The woman immediately arose from her bed and walked half a mile to be baptized. She then walked back again in her wet clothes. She was well from that time forth, was a mother a year later, and afterwards bore several children.

Elder Patten performed other miracles during his mission because of his faith and purity. He was obedient. He was courageous, and he was pure. What he did in Tennessee, you can do in Idaho and Oregon and Wyoming and Nevada and Georgia and Pennsylvania and New York and anywhere you have the purity to believe in Christ and live with total obedience. The Lord will be with you as your hearts are right.

Christ said, "Blessed are the pure in heart: for they shall see God" (Matthew 5:8). Purity brings not only the harvest but also spirituality. It makes possible our return to our Heavenly Father. "For what is a man profited, if he shall gain the whole world, and lose his own soul?" (Matthew 16:26).

Protect your own salvation. Be pure at all costs. Bring salvation to others. Teach with a pure spirit. Please don't be found guilty of rationalizing impure acts because of your ability to distort words. Live with exactness. The rewards will come.

Now elders and sisters, I want you to know that my wife and I love each of you very much. Our greatest desire is for your success and exaltation. May the Lord bless you with the harvest of your own soul as well of the souls of others, I pray in the name of Jesus Christ. Amen.

Love,

President Marbury

"I will so live that I may harvest my own soul, as well as the souls of others."

Precise Obedience

Dear Missionaries,

"Cease to be idle...cease to sleep longer than is needful" (D&C 88:124). Rest is needful. Idleness can be disastrous.

Santa Anna demonstrated this at the Battle of San Jacinto. Santa Anna's army numbered 1,600 Mexicans. Sam Houston, the commander-in-chief of the Texan army, commanded only 743 Texans. Santa Anna should have won, at least by virtue of numbers and experience, but he didn't. You see, Sam Houston knew of Santa Anna's insistence on his four o'clock siesta. He ordered his men to attack at precisely four o'clock—Santa Anna's naptime. The Mexicans were caught sleeping, and Texas became Texas in a battle that lasted less than twenty minutes.

We are pitted against the forces of Satan in a battle for the eternal lives of scores of individuals and families. Satan, unlike Santa Anna, will not be caught sleeping. Will we?

There is another important truth to be learned from the Battle of San Jacinto. General Sam Houston's troops were told the precise time to begin their attack. Against seemingly impossible odds, their only chance for victory depended on complete obedience to those instructions. The troops were obedient and, as a result, triumphant. Courage, training, conditioning, persistence, and valiance were important; nevertheless, the key to their success was that they started what they were sent to do at the appointed time.

You are soldiers in the Lord's army. Each day you are asked to begin your attack against the forces of Satan early in the day. You know the precise time. The Holy Ghost will leave the apartment at the appointed hour. Be with Him, and harvest.

Love,

President Marbury

"...Arise early, that your bodies and minds may be invigorated."

—D&C 88:124

Purity Includes Action

Dear Missionaries,

"Verily I say, men should be anxiously engaged in a good cause, and do many things of their own free will, and bring to pass much righteousness" (D&C 58:27). Thank you for being the wonderful missionaries you are. You are anxiously engaged, and the Lord is blessing you for it. It is an honor to be associated with you.

As our prophet, President Kimball, expressed his appreciation for all we do, he added that he hoped we would do more. I encourage each of us to plan a few (or many) more things we can do to lengthen our stride. In a stake conference in Soda Springs, Idaho, Elder Cuthbert quoted President Kimball as saying that if missionaries really understood the urgency of the work, they would run to every door. Some of you are doing that, and Heavenly Father is pleased with you for it.

May we never forget that we are more than gospel salespeople—we are gospel teachers. The salesperson is motivated by gain; the teacher is motivated by a genuine love and regard for others. The gospel salesperson sells numbers of baptisms; the gospel teacher brings a harvest of convert baptisms. We can increase our quantity while also increasing our quality. This is the Lord's way. It is the pure way.

We obtain the harvest by purifying ourselves as required to draw upon the powers of Heaven. This kind of purity is more

Purity Includes Action

than simply refraining from evil. It is action. It is being anxiously engaged. May the Lord bless you all as you are anxiously engaged in His service, I pray in the name of Jesus Christ. Amen.

Love,

President Marbury

"Purity includes action."

Put Away Childish Things

Dear Missionaries,

We read in 1 Corinthians 13:11 "...but when I became a man I put away childish things." Often we find men of age twelve and children of age sixty. Most of us are partially each. What makes a child a man? I believe the difference is in values. May I suggest three traits useful in making children men and good men great? Of course these traits apply equally to women as to men.

First on the list is a respect for deity. We show our respect by doing the things our Heavenly Father asks and expects of us. We pray night and morning. We're gracious. We think and speak clean thoughts. Since every member of the human race is a child of God, we also show our respect for Him by showing respect for His children. Do good deeds always. Every good deed is a press release for God.

Next is acceptance of responsibility. Children are always blaming circumstances or others for their lots in life. They are constantly saying that this or that isn't fair and that they won't do it. "That's somebody else's responsibility, not mine," they will say. The adult sees what needs to be done and goes about doing it. He graciously allows others to take credit for success and accepts all blame for failure. She is more concerned that good is done than with who gets the credit.

Finally, a man has the courage to persist. Children are quitters. Adults never quit. The child quits where the adult persists. The person who can't be beaten won't be beaten. Thomas Jefferson said that at the same time life is trying to educate us, it is sorting us. In other words, it is separating the men from the boys. As someone once said, "The coward never starts. The weak die on the way. Only the strong come through." Be strong. You are needed in the Kingdom.

Love,

President Marbury

"The coward never starts. The weak die on the way. Only the strong come through."

Put On Charity

Dear Missionaries,

"Above all things put on charity, which is the bond of perfectness." (Colossians 3:14)

Thank you all for being the great missionaries that you are. Above all else, I see a growth of charity throughout the mission. The Lord is rewarding this love with the harvest.

May I suggest we work on perfecting our charity each day? Perhaps the most significant way is to practice being grateful to the Lord for all he does for us. Joyce Buckner of Hartford City, Indiana, does this each night as she slips off to sleep. She goes through the alphabet, matching up the letters with words that describe the Savior and His love for us. "A," she says, stands for "Almighty," which He is. "B" is for "blessings," especially those we receive personally. "C" is for "calm," which He makes us feel. Joyce says that she's never had to find a word beginning with "X" or "Y" or "Z." She explains, "I've never been awake that long."

Put On Charity

As we develop thankful hearts, we put on charity and develop perfectness. You are doing just that, and the Lord is blessing you for it.

Love,

President Marbury

"The only greatness is unselfish love."

RECHARGE YOUR BATTERIES

Dear Missionaries,

   It's an honor to be serving in the same mission with each of you. You work hard, and you are pure. My wife and I love you all.
   One day last winter, as I was preparing to go to a meeting, my car wouldn't start. Mechanically, it was in good shape; it just had a dead battery. The missionaries soon arrived with jumper cables, which they attached to the strong battery in their car and then to the dead battery in mine. My car was running again in less than a minute.
   There are times in the lives of each of us when our spiritual batteries need recharging. A small charge is always needed every morning and evening. Larger charges are required in times of stress or unusual need. Prayer is the generator that recharges dead spiritual batteries. It costs no more to restore spiritual power through prayer today than it did twenty years ago, and there has been no cutback in service. Shouldn't we use it more often? Try it! You'll like it!

                                 Love,

                                President Marbury

"Prayer will recharge dead spiritual batteries."

Remove The Mountain

Dear Missionaries,

"...If ye have faith as a grain of a mustard seed, ye shall say unto this mountain, remove hence to yonder place; and it shall remove; and nothing shall be impossible unto you." (Matthew 17:20)

Few people believe that they can remove mountains, and as a result, few people do. The Lord has called you to remove the mountain. The Lord has called you to perform the miracle. He has called you to harvest. With sufficient faith—which includes hard work—you will do it. The Lord will bless you to succeed.

Love,

President Marbury

"Remove the mountain."

Repeat Success, Correct Mistakes

Dear Missionaries,

One of the blessings of serving a mission is the blessing of serving with so many souls who, like us, have made a free choice to give total commitment to the Savior for this part of their lives. In the process of serving, however, you will make mistakes—not on purpose, but you will make mistakes. The person who never makes a mistake probably isn't doing very much. It's these mistakes I would like to talk about.

We grow by repeating our successes and correcting our mistakes. Before we can correct our mistakes, we must recognize them. Sometimes these mistakes will be brought to our attention by others. When a guided missile is off course, it receives feedback to correct its course and bring it back on the right path. Likewise, when we err, we need corrective feedback to return us to the right. The correction may be painful at times, but it is needed and helpful. The Scriptures teach us, "For whom the Lord loveth He chasteneth" (Hebrews 12:6).

Although some negatives may belong to us, they are not us. We may make mistakes, but we are not mistakes. Whether we are wise or unwise is often determined by how we react to reproof. The Lord said in Proverbs 9:8, "Reprove not a scorner, lest he hate thee: rebuke a wise man, and he will love thee." Although we are not perfect, we are all striving for perfection. Growth comes one step at a time as we react wisely to correction.

Those we are called to teach also make mistakes. We change more easily as we are corrected with love. So will they. The most important change they can make immediately is to repent of their sins and be baptized. The most important work we can do immediately is to help convert those whom we teach in order that they may be baptized. May we do so with love in the name of Jesus Christ. Amen.

Love,

President Marbury

"We may make mistakes, but we not are mistakes."

Results Are According To Effort

Dear Missionaries,

You have the potential to become the finest missionaries in the world. How many of you have the ambition to aim above mediocrity? How many of you prefer to be great missionaries rather than simply missionaries who fulfilled a mission? You will be what you desire to be. Today, as someone else has said, is the first day of the rest of your life. Your results will be according to your efforts. You will not get a mansion for the price of a shack. Neither will you obtain celestial blessings for telestial efforts. There is a price to be paid for all we obtain. The blessings of the celestial kingdom await those who are willing to pay the price.

Step in front of the mirror. There, you see as one, two people—your best friend and your worst enemy. You see the conqueror and the conquered. You will conquer yourself, or you will be conquered by yourself. You influence others as you first conquer yourself.

The easiest road is the road that allows us to do whatever we feel like doing. It leads to a dead end. A little extra effort will take us to the foot of the mountain. Reaching the peak requires persistent hard work. The disobedient road is the telestial road. The obedient road is the terrestrial road. Celestial rewards require obedience and a little (or a lot) more. The blessings equal the price paid.

Every decision requires the sacrifice of some alternative. The choice is yours. You may sacrifice a harvest for "doing your own thing," or you may sacrifice "doing your own thing" for a harvest. You and those to whom the Lord has sent you to serve will be blessed accordingly.

Love,

President Marbury

"I know my results will be in accordance with my efforts. I will multiply my efforts."

Self-Denial

Dear Missionaries,

Elder Welker recently sent me an article by Elder Vaughn J. Featherstone of the First Quorum of the Seventy. The article was on self-denial, and I'm grateful to him for sending it. Among other things, it quoted Clarence Scharer saying,

> The real qualities of leadership are found in those who are willing to sacrifice for the sake of objectives great enough to demand their wholehearted allegiance. Simply holding a position of leadership does not make a man a leader...If you would be a real leader, you must endure loneliness...If you would be a real leader, you must endure weariness. Leadership requires vision.

Another person was quoted as saying, "Leaders need to submit themselves to a stricter discipline than is expected of others. Those who are first in place must be first in merit."

You are called on this mission to prepare yourself and others for leadership in the Kingdom of God. The very fact that you are here is evidence of your potential greatness. You achieve this quality of greatness as you lose yourselves in the service of others. Elder Featherstone also tells of a student at Harvard who told the dean that he failed to complete an assignment because he

Self-Denial

wasn't feeling very well. The dean replied, "I think in time you may perhaps find that most of the work in the world is done by people who aren't feeling very well."

The principle of self-denial is a true one. Sacrifice brings forth the blessings of Heaven. May all of us serve our missions in ways that will bring forth many blessings, I pray in the name of Jesus Christ. Amen.

Love,

President Marbury

"Those who are first in place must be first in merit."

Self-Discipline Is A Key To Success

Dear Missionaries,

"Behold, the Lord requireth the heart and a willing mind; and the willing and obedient shall eat the good of the land of Zion in these last days." (D&C 64:34)

Although perfection in this life is not required to obtain promised blessings from the Lord, the Lord does require obedience and a willing heart. Another way of saying this is that self-discipline is a key to success.

Be strong in the hard moments. When Satan tempts you to relax, be strong. When you begin to be distracted by girlfriends or boyfriends, be strong. When you find yourself rationalizing behavior that leads to failure, be strong. You are representatives of Jesus Christ. You are children of God. Be grateful for who you are and who you represent. You are on the Lord's team. You are a winner.

While others of lesser courage despair, you will persist until you conquer. Through you, the Lord will have His victory over Satan. I know the Lord is leading us to the harvest. You and I are blessed to have this opportunity to be part of it. Work. Convert. Baptize. May the Lord bless you.

                      Love,

                      President Marbury

"Work. Convert. Baptize."

Serious Covenants Made To The Lord

Dear Missionaries,

I am impressed today to write of the serious covenants we all made to the Lord in coming on our missions. We covenanted to serve with all our hearts, might, minds, and strength. We covenanted to lift, to build, to serve with an eye single to the glory of God. We covenanted to be faithful in the little things as well as things of seemingly greater importance. We covenanted to love and follow our leaders.

The work of the Lord is serious—too serious to allow the pettiness of temper and criticism to impede its success. May we renew, today, the covenants made to Heavenly Father to serve Him above ourselves. May we resolve to make the sacrifices that go with obedience.

My wife and I love the Savior, and we love you. With all our hearts we desire to see you succeed. Jesus said, "For whosoever will save his life shall lose it: and whosoever will lose his life for my sake shall find it" (Matthew 16:25). In saving false pride by doing things "our way," we lose. In losing our life in total service to the Master, we find salvation. That we may find life through total service to the Master, I pray in the name of Jesus Christ. Amen.

Love,

President Marbury

"I will make the sacrifices that go with obedience."

SET YOUR GOALS

Dear Missionaries,

Have you set your goals for the year? If not, here are some suggestions for setting them. If you have set them, perhaps you may want to review them in light of these ideas.

Goals should desirably fall into categories—activity goals and achievement goals. Achievement will be based on activity. Goals should be reasonable, believable, and your own, not someone else's. There may be minimum standards of activity set by others, such as fifteen discussions per week, but it will still be your decision to perform at, below, or above the minimum. Of course activity at or below the minimum brings at or below minimum achievement.

I would begin by deciding on achievement goals that I believe I can achieve beyond any reasonable doubt. Then I would decide what activities are necessary to reach them and make certain I do those activities. Next I would ask myself, "Are there ways I can improve my effectiveness to achieve more? Do I want to do it? Am I willing to do it? Will I do it?" If the answer is yes to all four questions, then I would increase my goals. If the answer to any one is no, I would leave my goals where they are for the present. If I have strong doubts about my original goals, I may temporarily lower them with the idea that I will reach some more intermediate goals first, and then reach for higher ones.

Set Your Goals

Although I may have one very high and lofty goal, one which may take a month, a year, or a lifetime to achieve, I will have many smaller and short-term ones. I like to succeed. I like to win. I like to feel good about myself, so I always set one or more goals every day that I know I will reach and that will also bring me one step closer to my primary long-term goal. Each time I reach one of these goals, in my own mind I have succeeded. I am a winner, and I feel good about myself.

Temporary failure is often part of achievement. I will reach some goals every day, but maybe not every goal always. I am better than others at some things, but not in everything. I will excel where I have special talents and work to improve where I have weaknesses. Above all, I will be totally honest with myself and with the Lord in all I do—and I will never quit. God bless you to do likewise.

Love,

President Marbury

"I will be totally honest with myself and with the Lord in all I do—and I will never quit."

Six Commitment Principles

Dear Missionaries,

We have recently been focusing on missionary commitment. Six principles will significantly increase your success in bringing people to know the gospel. They are:

1. Sanctify yourselves.
2. Commit a local member every day to have an investigator taught in his or her home.
3. Use the referral dialogue in every first discussion and obtain referrals with every discussion.
4. Challenge those you teach, in every discussion, to qualify themselves for baptism.
5. Baptize on a regular basis.
6. Invite the nonmember friends of new converts to the baptismal service at every baptism.

Commitment is a key to success—both yours and the investigators. Commit yourself to following the above principles now. In addition become skilled at committing others. One successful approach consists of beginning with prayer, presenting a spiritual thought, asking for the commitment while the spirit is present, and closing with prayer. Ask commitment questions in such a way that a reasonably sincere person cannot say "no."

Remember, we are only asking for commitments that will bless the lives of those making the commitments.

One way to commit an investigator could be to use Matthew 3:13–17. After reading the Scripture, you could ask the investigator, "How would you feel if God said He was well pleased with you? What did Christ do to please God? Would you like to please your Heavenly Father? What should you do to please Him?" Notice that a sincere person can give only one answer to each of these questions.

A local member could be approached with questions such as these, "What does D&C 15:6 say is the thing of most worth to you? How would you feel having many souls tell you how much they love you for your part in bringing them into the Kingdom of God? Which of your friends would you like to prepare for us to teach in your home? When would you like us to come?"

May the Lord bless you to harvest. I know he will.

Love,

President Marbury

"Why not go out on a limb? That's where the fruit is."

The Spirit Knows No Handicap—First Thanksgiving

Dear Missionaries,

On September 16, 1620, a little ship called the Mayflower, crowed with 102 passengers and 20 crew members, set sail from Plymouth, England. The ship was only about ninety feet long and twenty-five feet wide, but the Pilgrims had a purpose—religious freedom—and a destination—the New World! Land was spotted after sixty-six days of sailing. For another three months, the Pilgrims lived on the Mayflower while shelters were constructed on shore.

THE FIRST THANKSGIVING

The first winter was hard. Many died of cold and starvation. Many others lived—because they learned to make friends. Native Americans, called savages by some but saviors by the starving Pilgrims, taught the newcomers how to plant corn, find eels and clams, and get food from the wilderness. With the help of their new Native American friends, crops of corn, wheat, barley, and vegetables were planted the following spring. The first harvest was abundant. The Native Americans and Pilgrims feasted for three days. Each succeeding year, one day was set aside for thanksgiving.

George Washington, in 1789, called for a national day of thanks in honor of America's victory in the War of Independence. Seventy-four years later, in 1863, Abraham Lincoln proclaimed the last Thursday in November to be the national holiday we now celebrate each year as Thanksgiving Day.

THANKSGIVING TODAY

Wherever we are, whatever we do, we have much to be thankful for. We are alive. We have a loving Heavenly Father. We are limited only by what we fail to conceive and believe. We are constantly blessed according to our eternal needs and personal worthiness to receive blessings. When we lack in personal worthiness, we need only to repent to qualify again.

Happiness is a matter of attitude, not condition. David Schwartz tells of a friend who is an excellent golfer, despite the fact that one of his arms was amputated several years ago. When asked how he developed such a near-perfect style with just one arm, his friend replied, "Well, it's my experience that the right attitude with one arm will beat the wrong attitude with two arms every time." Regardless of who you are or what you were, you can be what you want to be.

THE SPIRIT KNOWS NO HANDICAP

In contemplating our personal blessings, lest we regard them too lightly, consider Becky Reeve. On November 16, 1962, Becky Reeve was a missionary serving in New Mexico. There was a light snow that day, and as she drove with her companion to zone conference, the slick road captured another victim. Her car spun out of control. Sliding off the road, it rolled two and a half times, coming to rest upside down. Sister Reeve was thrown out of the car, landing hard on the back of her head some fifty feet away. Her neck was broken. The fifth and sixth vertebrae in her neck were dislocated, leaving her paralyzed from the neck down. Her internal organs were also paralyzed. Near death, she was carefully loaded into an ambulance by emergency workers and sped toward the hospital.

What did Sister Reeve do on the trip to the hospital? Near death, and deep into shock, she taught the first discussion to the attendants!

Despite physical paralysis, Becky Reeve, daughter of Elder Rex Reeve of the First Quorum of the Seventy, maintains a pleasant countenance and positive attitude. She reminds those of us of lesser faith that unless we teach differently "The spirit knows no handicap."

"Greater love hath no man than this, that a man lay down his life for his friends" (John 15:13). Christ died for us. Shall we not live for him? If Becky Reeve can teach the gospel though paralyzed, shall we who have all our health do less? God bless us all to express our thanks by rendering total service to the kingdom.

Love,

President Marbury

"The spirit knows no handicap."

—Becky Reeve

Spirit Of Christmas

Dear Missionaries,

"And the angel said unto them, Fear not: for behold I bring you good tidings of great joy, which shall be to all people. For unto you is born this day in the city of David a Savior, which is Christ the Lord." (Luke 2:10-11)

I can feel the spirit of the mission lift as Christmas is upon us. The Savior talked of purity, and you are following His example. The Savior set an example of work, and you are doing likewise. The Savior's entire life was a life of service, and you have this mission to serve without ceasing.

Your weekly letters are uplifting, and I sense an increasing desire to follow the Savior. Comments like these are common: "I will go for greatness." "I will not be content to say that something must be done. I will do something." "I will pray for a good harvest, but keep plowing." "I will live what I teach." "I will be an example to match the message."

Dear Missionaries

The Lord is pleased with your diligence and righteous desires. As we baptize this Christmas, may we dedicate each baptism as our gift to the Christ child.

Love,

President Marbury

"Go for greatness!"

—Elder Raymond Roberge

The Successful Never Give Up

Dear Missionaries,

"Judge not, that ye be not judged." (Matthew 7:1)
Christ gave this counsel to His apostles with the added warning that they would be judged according to how they judge others. I am convinced this counsel applies to our judgment of ourselves as well as our judgment of others. Sometimes we play ourselves down when we have the ability to accomplish a thing as well as or better than the seemingly most qualified. Knowledge alone doesn't make for success; it must be applied.

One would think that one would have to hold a college degree to be president of the United States—yet George Washington, Grover Cleveland, Abraham Lincoln, and Harry S. Truman never attended college. Orville and Wilbur Wright never completed high school. Thomas Edison, one of the greatest inventors of all time, never even completed grade school, nor did US bandleader and composer John Philip Sousa or writers Charles Dickens and Mark Twain. Albert Einstein once flunked math. Joseph Smith was also called "unlearned."

Thomas Jefferson had a speech defect. Helen Keller was blind. James Madison was an epileptic. Franklin D. Roosevelt could not walk. John Adams had frequent attacks off extreme depression. The list goes on and on.

Richard Bach's novel *Jonathan Livingston Seagull* was refused by eighteen publishers before MacMillan agreed to accept it and quietly issued 7,500 copies. In five years, more than 7,000,000 copies had been sold. Animator and film producer Walt Disney was forced to declare bankruptcy in 1923 and owned nothing more than a pair of pants, a coat, a shirt, two pairs of underwear, two pairs of socks, and some miscellaneous drawing equipment.

These people all had one virtue in common: a belief in themselves and in what they were doing. They didn't judge themselves as disadvantged and they weren't. May the Lord bless you to do likewise.

Love,

President Marbury

"He who learns but does not think is lost. He who thinks but does not learn is in great danger."

The Sun And The Wind

Dear Missionaries,

"And be ye kind one to another, tenderhearted, forgiving one another, even as God for Christ's sake has forgiven you." (Ephesians 4:32)

You continue to do well each day. I am blessed to be able to work with you. You work hard. You study regularly. You are diligent. As you continue in the work of the Lord, I would leave with you this thought: be kind. It takes a unique kind of strength, and self-will, to exhibit kindness under many circumstances, but I ask you to be strong enough to always be kind.

There is a story about an argument between the sun and the wind as to who was stronger. The wind suggested a contest. He pointed to a man wearing an overcoat and walking along a city sidewalk. The winner of the contest would be the one who could remove the man's overcoat.

The wind howled and blew cold, stormy air, tugging at the man's overcoat and causing him to stagger from the power of the fierce gale. But the more forceful the wind, the tighter the man held his coat about him. After several hours, the wind gave up.

Now it was the sun's turn. Coming from behind the clouds, the sun smiled kindly on the man in the overcoat. As the warm air embraced him, the man smiled, wiped his brow, and removed his coat. "You see," explained the sun to the wind, "gentleness and friendliness are always stronger than fury and force."

Kindness is among the greatest of virtues. It brings happiness to both the giver and the receiver. It uplifts. It motivates. It comforts. Kindness wins friends and influences people. Kindness is never out of fashion. It is the mark of a winner. Let it be your trademark also.

Love,

President Marbury

"Be kind."

Take The Lord's Side On Every Issue

Dear Missionaries,

At a recent stake conference, Elder Bruce R. McConkie was quoted as saying, "To be valiant in the testimony of Jesus is to take the Lord's side on every issue." Elder McConkie concluded by reminding us not to take the Church cafeteria style. We can't just take what we want and leave the rest. You, each of you, is called to set the example. You are called to make the difference.

I'm Grateful For You

I'm grateful for you. I'm grateful to be associated with people filled with your devotion, dedication, and spirituality. You have loved thousands of converts into the Church. You work together as a team of local members and full-time missionaries, showing your love for the Savior and sharing His message. You forgive our weaknesses while constantly strengthening yourselves. You are anxiously engaged in personalizing and giving away copies of the Book of Mormon. You regularly open your homes so that families you have friendshipped may be taught the gospel. You are great.

I NEED YOUR HELP

Like you, I love Christ and Heavenly Father with all my heart. I have been called to help this mission reach its missionary potential. I pledge to you my total commitment in this. Please help me help you.

We reach our potential as we grow in serving the Lord with exactness. Will you do these things in your stakes and wards?

1. Help every family make a positive commitment to missionary activity and commit not less than 20 percent of your families to love another family into the church this year.
2. Personalize not less than one copy of the Book of Mormon for every member of your congregation by having them include their testimonies with their signatures on the inside covers of the copies of the Book of Mormon. If they wish, members can also include photographs of their families.
3. Stake and ward priesthood and auxiliary leaders, set the example by giving missionary referrals to the full-time missionaries and make plans for those referrals to be taught in your home.

THANK YOU

It has been said that all that is required to make us unmindful of what we owe for our blessings is that we should receive the blessings often and regularly. You have blessed me often and regularly since my calling to this great mission. I promise you not to be unmindful of these blessings. Thanks again for all you do.

Socrates said, "Let him that would move the world, first move himself." The Lord told us that the thing of most worth to us is to bring souls unto Him (D&C 15:6). Shall we not first move ourselves to share the gospel? Are we really giving priority to that which is of most worth? Are we careful never to let those things that matter least get in the way of those things that matter most? To make the difference, we must do things differently, greater, and more effectively. I know you can do it. God bless you and thank you.

Love,

President Marbury

"To be valiant in the testimony of Jesus is to take the Lord's side on every issue."

—Bruce R. McConkie

THE TEACHINGS OF NEPHI

Dear Missionaries,

You are growing spiritually every day, and my wife and I are grateful for you. To paraphrase Helaman 10:4, "Blessed art thou Elders and Sisters, for the things which thou hast done." To ensure continued blessings, may we all follow the example that Nephi explains in the remainder of the verse.

DECLARE THE WORD UNWEARIEDLY

Work every available minute. See that your life is focused, dedicated, and disciplined. With all the infinite possibilities of the Kingdom of God before you, don't settle for a little patch of ground at the foot of the mountain. Climb until you reach the summit. Remember, even the woodpecker owes his success to the fact that he uses his head and keeps pecking away until he finishes the job he starts.

FEAR NOT

Know you will succeed. You are made in God's image; therefore, nothing is inferior about you. God doesn't make junk. Fear not those who would belittle the truth. Someone said one of the greatest devices of the devil is to fasten names of contempt on certain virtues and thus fill weak souls with a foolish fear of appearing too good should they desire to practice such virtues. Rather than praying for tasks equal to your powers, pray for powers equal to your tasks. Speak in positive terms. If you say a thing often enough, your subconscious will turn it into fact.

SEEK GOD'S WILL AND KEEP HIS COMMANDMENTS

Lose yourself in the work. Keep every commandment precisely. Never rationalize with the Lord. Be greater than minimum missionaries.

REMEMBER YOUR TOTAL RELIANCE ON THE LORD

Someone very wise, whose name I do not know, said that prayer is often the course of last resort when in fact it should be the first. In this day of inflation, it costs no more to send a prayer today than it did hundreds of years ago, and there has been no cutback in service. Considering the help available and the bargain it represents, it's surprising we don't pray more often. May we do so, I pray in the name of Jesus Christ. Amen.

Love,

President Marbury

"Never rationalize with the Lord."

Tenth Anniversary Of Our Baptism

Dear Missionaries,

How so many of you knew, I don't know, but this past week my wife and I received dozens of cards congratulating us on the tenth anniversary of our baptisms. We were baptized September 4, 1969. Thanks to all who wrote.

As I reflect on our baptisms, I find myself forever grateful to the many missionaries and members who continued to be our friends while we slowly gained the necessary testimony to request baptism. We studied the gospel for many years before our baptisms. I attended early-morning seminary for two years before being baptized. The love, friendship, and refusal of many people to give up on us finally bore fruit.

The Lord loves us all. He never gives up. While some are ready to be taught now, all are ready to be loved now. May we teach those who are ready and love those still preparing until they, too, become receptive to the gospel, I pray in the name of Jesus Christ. Amen.

Love,

President Marbury

"While some are ready to be taught now, all are ready to be loved now."

That We May All Be One—A Student's Prayer

Dear Missionaries,

In perhaps one of the greatest prayers ever recorded, Jesus requested "That they may all be one; as thou, Father art in me, and I in Thee, that they also may be one in us: that the world may believe that thou hast sent me" (John 17:21). Again and again God's eternal command to His people is "be one."

ONE MISSIONARY PROGRAM

One of our great opportunities to show we are one is in missionary work. The mission, the stake, the ward, and the family work as one team to bring converts into the Lord's kingdom. We are not carrying out multiple missionary programs. We work together in the one missionary program of the Church.

The most effective way to find people to teach is for families to become friends with their nonmember neighbors and then invite them to be taught by the missionaries. The most effective way to teach is for a stake missionary to team up with a full-time missionary. Each full-time missionary should work with a stake missionary, where possible, every evening except Monday and during the daytime when possible. Obviously, stake and full-time missionaries share all of their contacts and investigators with each other so that they may all work together and "be one" as taught by Jesus Christ.

ONE GOAL—EXALTATION FOR ALL

The story is told of a young minister who asked all who wanted to go to Heaven to raise their hands. When all but one hand went up, the minister inquired concerning this one person's hesitation. "I want to go to Heaven someday," came the reply, "I just thought you were getting up a load to leave right now."

Life is precious. Leaving it prematurely is never desirable. While we still have life, we have the opportunity, and obligation, to lift others so that their lives extend beyond the grave, exalted with their Heavenly Father. As we anxiously build exaltation for others, we never have to worry about our own.

ONE TESTIMONY—GOD LIVES, JESUS IS THE CHRIST

The most powerful personal weapon we have in the work of converting souls is our own testimony. A testimony is the purest form of human communication. It helps others feel less like strangers. People everywhere hunger for something fixed and unchangeable. We have it in the gospel. Testify of it often.

Some time ago, before joining the Church of Jesus Christ of Latter-day Saints, I wrote a sonnet about my desire to know the truth and my determination to follow it. It was written in the form of a prayer. I am including it here in hope that it will be meaningful to you. As I was a college student at the time, I called it "A Student's Prayer."

That We May All Be One—A Student's Prayer

A Student's Prayer

Dear Father, prod my mind and heart awake
Till all my senses keen within my soul
Unite in one great effort to behold
The marvels You created for my sake.

Dear Father, grant me wisdom, knowledge and
Ability to use them in a way
That strengthens someone's character each day
And helps them find Your all-inspiring hand.

Eternal gratitude I pledge, oh Lord,
For all the grief You took because of me.
I'll work to take my place in that great chord
Which harmonizes all mankind with Thee.

My mind and heart I shall forever lend
To serve what way I may, dear Lord. Amen.

Love,

President Marbury

"My mind and heart I shall forever lend
Serve what way I may, dear Lord. Amen."

THINK UPHILL THOUGHTS

Dear Missionaries,

Positive thoughts grow stronger with constant repetition. Believe in yourself, your work, and your Savior—now! Let your every action reflect confidence. Think uphill thoughts. You cannot climb uphill thinking downhill thoughts. Never let yesterday use up today. Be the best. Think the best. Refuse to accept the judgment of those who are resigned to be average. "For as he thinketh in his heart, so is he" (Proverbs 23:7).

Elders and sisters, my wife and I love you with all of our hearts. We are grateful the Lord sent you, the finest missionaries in the world, to us. We know you can establish a Zion mission. We know that as you visit the homes of those within this mission, we will harvest because of your purity. May the Lord bless you with health, strength, and happiness as you serve Him.

Love,

President Marbury

"Today's dream will become tomorrow's reality."

This Christmas, And Always, We Serve The Savior

Dear Missionaries,

Where love is, the Savior is pleased. This is the season of love, and it is the time of year more dedicated to the Savior worldwide than all other times. The gospel is a gospel of love. As we demonstrate our love for the Savior through others, we will present him with an abundant harvest.

We are on our missions to serve the Savior. We are not here to seek position or to magnify ourselves. We are not here to find fault with our companions or fellow missionaries. The weaknesses of those around us should have little influence on our own faithfulness. We are here to serve the Savior.

The Savior is asking us to help Him make this a better world. He knew of our weaknesses when He came to this Earth. He knew we were not worthy of His sacrifice, but He lovingly suffered for us because He loved us. The less He was loved, the harder He worked so that all might learn to love one another through His example. He never spoke a word to belittle others; complain of how other treated Him unjustly; or suggest that because no one else was perfect, He need not be perfect either. Christ only asked that we follow His example and repent when necessary in order to receive His blessings.

Elders and sisters, remember that you are working for the Savior this Christmas. When you are tempted to watch TV, attend evening movies, sleep late, complain, or speak unkindly of your fellow missionaries, remember whom you serve. The Savior would have you pure. The Savior would have you baptize abundantly, since baptism is the only way your contacts can gain celestial exaltation. May our righteous example please the Savior this Christmas and always.

Love,

President Marbury

"Remember whom you serve."

This Christmas, Increase The Spirit Of Love

Dear Missionaries,

Visiting you in your district meetings and being with you in your recent zone conferences were good experiences for me. You are fine representatives of the Savior.

I have been impressed recently that the most important thing we can do at present is to increase the spirit of love throughout the mission. We all need to feel and express more love for the Savior, each other, and those we are called to teach. Will you help?

Call morning can be a beginning. As you give your reports to your leaders, add words of thanks for their leadership. Leaders, lift those who report to you. Let your voices communicate excitement. Let your words communicate praise for worthy accomplishments and confidence that needed improvements will come quickly. Let no discouraging words leave your lips. Let us speak kind words at all times.

Love is best demonstrated by good works and by our many convert baptisms for the Savior. Commit your investigators with sweet boldness. Motivate and encourage your fellow missionaries to do likewise. You are engaged in a great work.

Dear Missionaries

Do it with love and enthusiasm. Merry Christmas!

Love,

President Marbury

"How beautiful a day can be when kindness touches it."

Thomas And Henry Ward Beecher

Dear Missionaries,

The story is told of how the brother of Henry Ward Beecher, Thomas Beecher, was once asked to substitute for his famous brother at a church service. During the opening hymn, several members of the congregation, realizing that Thomas, rather than his famous brother Henry, would be the speaker, began to move to the nearest exit. Stopping the service, Thomas announced, "Those who came to worship my brother may leave now. Those who came to worship God are invited to join me in the singing of the rest of the hymn."

This story reminds me of our need to focus our attention on the worship of God and of Jesus Christ rather than on less significant things. We are all here to do what the Savior would do in our place. Who we serve is just as important as who we are. We serve best by being pure and baptizing Heavenly Father's children so that they can return to Him. You are doing that with greatness. God bless you for it.

Love,

President Marbury

"Who we serve is just as important as who we are."

Three Meetings

Dear Missionaries,

While I was working as an engineer in South Georgia, my firm had the opportunity to design a pumping station that would be located a few feet from a large dike. The dike served to protect the surrounding property against floodwaters from the adjacent river. As construction of the pumping station neared completion, we found a defective valve on a storm drainage pipe going through the dam. If the valve broke, floodwaters would reach the pumping station and destroy thousands of dollars of electrical equipment. Fixing the valve was a simple matter, and we reported it to the maintenance department.

About six months later, we noticed that no work had yet been done to fix the defective valve. Again we reported the need, stressing the low cost to fix the valve and the high cost of repairing any flood damage. Several more times we stressed the need to do something. Each time, those in charge of maintenance listened to us attentively—and did nothing.

In time the floods came. The valve had not been repaired, and thousands of dollars were lost in damages. Frustrated, we approached the maintenance department.

"Why didn't you do something?"

"We did."

"Well, what did you do?"

"We had three meetings!"

Get the point? No matter how many meetings or how many good intentions, until action is taken, nothing is accomplished. As you plan your work, don't forget to work your plan. May the Lord bless you to plan and work effectively.

Love,

President Marbury

"Good intentions are like crying babies; they should be carried out."

—Brigham Young

To All There Is A Season

Dear Missionaries,

Ecclesiastes 3:1 reads, "To every thing there is a season, and a time to every purpose under the heaven." The Lord has set a timetable for the accomplishment of all His purposes. Even the flowering plants follow a set timetable in yielding their nectar to the honeybees. The wild mustard is ready at about nine o'clock in the morning, as are certain types of dandelions. The blue cornflower is prepared near eleven o'clock. Bees visit red clover around one o'clock. Later in the afternoon, at three o'clock or so, the viper's bugloss is ready.

Although the gospel is available to all at any time, there are times when prospective members are more receptive. Families, newly moving into a neighborhood, have an immediate need for friendship and the gospel. Newlyweds and new parents often accept the gospel quickly. At the loss of a loved one, the message of family life together in the hereafter provides needed comfort. Personal tragedy awakens in many the need for greater spirituality. Those alone and with few friends yearn for the close associations gained through membership in the Church.

When families are prepared for the gospel—when referrals are given, when the time is right—they probably will be golden for the next two or three days, silver for the next two or three weeks, and copper after that. Timing is important.

Work on the Lord's timetable. Pray to know what it is. The Lord has told us, "Behold, I will hasten my work in its time" (D&C 88:73). The time is now.

Love,

President Marbury

"This time, like all times, is a very good one, if we but know what to do with it."

—Ralph Waldo Emerson

Tribute To James Melvin Weaver

Dear Missionaries,

On Sunday, April 26, 1981, at about seven thirty in the morning, Elder James Melvin Weaver returned to Heavenly Father. He had served as executive secretary to the Idaho Pocatello and Boise mission presidency since 1978. No man ever served more faithfully.

Elder Weaver was born to a farm family in Hartford County, Maryland, on December 26, 1907. At the age of seven he was driving a milk wagon and sharing men's work with his dad. By the age of fourteen, he was running an entire farm. Hard work was a basic part of his character. Everything he did, he did well and with complete dedication. He never believed good was enough; he only believed in being best. During his younger years he was a professional boxer. He had thirty-three bouts in his professional career. He never lost a bout. He loved flying and held a private pilot's license. He was considered one of the best foremen ever to work with Bell Telephone.

Elder Weaver's great love was the Church and the missionaries. When called to serve as the mission executive secretary, he stated he wanted to serve full time, and from that day forth he labored fifty to seventy-five hours each week, seeking to further the success of the mission. I remember one missionary who was asked to work with Elder Weaver for a couple of weeks. His name was

Elder Joseph Carlson. Elder Carlson was concerned about being able to work hard with a seventy-one-year-old companion. At the end of the first week, Elder Carlson asked me to ask the seventy-one-year-old man to slow down. He said Elder Weaver would get him up at five thirty each morning to run together for five miles before breakfast. After a quick breakfast, they would tract most of the day, running from door to door, and teach discussions until late in the evening. Elder Carlson said, "President, I can't keep up with him!"

In the last week of his life, Elder Weaver was teaching the gospel from his hospital bed to the person in the bed next to his. He never complained. He never criticized. He never asked for an easier assignment. We will all miss this great man.

Love,

President Marbury

"And, if you keep my commandments and endure to the end you shall have eternal life, which gift is the greatest of all the gifts of God."

—D&C 14:7

True Conversions

Dear Missionaries,

In a recent letter, the first presidency reemphasized the necessity of obtaining true conversions as we baptize souls into the Kingdom. They again stressed that the requirements for baptism are set forth in D&C 20:37. They also specified some additional requirements for the preparation for baptism. Effective immediately, you are asked to ensure that every investigator meets the following requirements prior to baptism:

1. Be taught all standard missionary discussions and come to a knowledge of the Savior.
2. Attend two or more Sunday Church meetings (such as sacrament and Sunday school, Sunday school and priesthood, or sacrament and a baptism), and feel a unity and oneness with Church members.
3. Meet the bishop or branch president. (When this is not practical due to their absence, the investigator may be introduced to one of their counselors.)
4. Repent and commit to live all the commandments of God.

May I also remind you that President Kimball added, "We are at last ready to move forward in a major way...We have paused on some plateaus long enough." There is no lessening of our commitment to greatly increase the number of convert baptisms; however, never forget that the goal is more than just baptisms—it is convert baptisms.

In baseball we score by going from first base to second and third and then to home. If we fail to touch any base, we fail to score. Champions achieve high scores and do it in the proper way. You are called of God to be champions. I know you are.

Love,

President Marbury

"I am called of God to be a champion."

Truth Needs No Disguise

Dear Missionaries,

Proverbs 8:7 reads, "For my mouth shall speak truth." This admonition is repeated in Zechariah 8:16 in these words, "These are the things that ye shall do; Speak ye every man the truth to his neighbor." Ether 3:12 records, "...Yea, Lord, I know that thou speaketh the truth, for thou art a God of truth, and canst not lie."

Truthfulness is a quality every missionary should develop. Sometimes, in an attempt to accomplish good works, we may be tempted to disguise the truth; this is not the Lord's way. We need never say, "Bring your nonmember friends to this discussion, but don't tell them it is a Church meeting or that we will talk about baptism." What you have to teach does lead to baptism.

We likewise have no need to say, "We just want to talk about religion, we aren't trying to get you to change." We are trying to change the lives of all whom we contact—so that they may lead richer and fuller lives.

Complete honesty in all things is the Lord's way and will bring the greatest results. We carry a message of love and truth to the world. This message is about the visit of our Heavenly Father and his son Jesus Christ to the Earth in our time. We desire others to hear it so that they may share with us the happiness it brings. When they come to know it is true, they can begin to obtain this happiness by being baptized into the Lord's Church.

We are not afraid to speak the truth plainly. As our faith grows stronger, we develop a greater ability to bless the lives of others. Go forth with truth and power—and baptize. Commit a family this week. The Lord will help you.

> Love,
>
> President Marbury

"Truth needs no disguise."

Turn Problems Into Opportunities

Dear Missionaries,

"Have not I commanded thee? Be strong and of a good courage; be not afraid, neither be thou dismayed: for the Lord thy God is with thee wheresoever thou goest." (Joshua 1:9)

W. Clement Stone, co-author of *Success through a Positive Mental Attitude* and other motivational books, has been quoted often as saying, "You have a problem? That's good!" With this philosophy he is teaching that anything can be turned into good, that any problem can be turned into an advantage, when faith is joined with positive thinking.

Theodore Roosevelt's 1912 convention speech was about to be printed in three million copies when the chairman of his campaign committee learned that document's photos of Roosevelt and his running mate, Governor Hiram Johnson of California, were not approved for use in the printing. Using them without permission would result in a fine of one dollar per copy, or three million dollars. Lesser men would have complained about oversight and shut down the presses in disgust and defeat. Not this campaign chairman.

Quickly, the following telegram was wired to the Chicago studio that had taken the photo: "Planning to issue three million copies of Roosevelt speech with pictures of Roosevelt and Johnson on cover. Great publicity opportunity for photographers. What will you pay us to use your photographs?"

This reply was received an hour later: "Appreciate opportunity, but can pay only two hundred fifty dollars."

Does it seem that you are always getting the lemons in life? Make lemonade out of them. Do others eat the fruit, leaving you with only the seeds? Plant them. Cultivate them. Harvest them, and your fruit will exceed the one by a hundred fold. Do it. My wife and I love you all.

Love,

President Marbury

"You have a problem? That's good!"

—W. CLEMENT STONE

Unselfish Service In The Animal Kingdom

Dear Missionaries,

"And behold, I tell you these things that ye may learn wisdom; that ye may learn that when ye are in the service of your fellow beings ye are only in the service of your God." (Mosiah 2:17)

The animal kingdom provides many examples of dedicated, unselfish service. The dog is known as "man's best friend" for good reason. Barry, a St. Bernard who lived in Switzerland from 1800 until 1814, dedicated his entire life to saving snowbound travelers. During his fourteen years of life, he rescued more than forty people from what otherwise would have been frozen graves.

A canary named Bibs brought honor to her kind. She was owned by an elderly woman of Hermitage, Tennessee, known as Old Aunt Tess. When Old Aunt Tess fell, severely injuring herself, Bibs flew to a neighboring house and banged against the window until she aroused the neighbor's attention. With the neighbor's help, Old Aunt Tess survived. Bibs died. In saving her master's life, she exhausted herself with excessive tapping.

Jack was a chacma baboon belonging to James Wide, a legless railroad switchman in South Africa. Such was Jack's intelligence and love for his master that each day he pushed the wheelchair-bound James Wide to work. As time went by, Jack learned to do small chores in the signal box and, later, to operate the signal levers by himself. Jack gave continuous service to his master for nine years until he died in 1890.

If animals can devote their lives to serving their masters, who are imperfect, should not we devote our life to serving our Master, who is perfect and gave his life for us? We show our love for the Savior by the way we serve. How much love will we show on our mission?

Love,

President Marbury

"The only ones among you who will be really happy are those who will have sought and found how to serve."

—Albert Schweitzer

Unwavering Standards

Dear Missionaries,

"Thus saith the Lord God: Behold I will lift up mine hand to the Gentiles, and set up my standard to the people." (I Nephi 21:22)

Within each of us, there are unwavering standards—standards below which we will not fall, regardless of the rewards or consequences. At least there should be these standards. One measure of an individual's character is the quality of these standards.

Would you rob a bank for $5,000? What about shoplifting? What about robbing another individual of his or her good name? How about another's time?

What are your standards for grooming? Would you go for a month without bathing or fixing your hair? Would you be content to wear dirty clothes every day? Are you willing to represent the Lord with unpressed clothes or unshined shoes?

How honest are you? Do you honestly teach all the discussions you report? Would you tell a lie to keep from looking bad in the eyes of a friend or acquaintance? Do you work as hard when the weather is cold as when it is more comfortable? Do you visit members to be fed or to teach investigators? Are your decisions based on what is best for the missionary effort or on what is most pleasant and enjoyable? Do you spend time searching for music tapes to purchase or for families to baptize? Are the majority of your thoughts missionary oriented or world oriented?

Standards of action do not remain the same. They may be raised or lowered. What are yours now? What will they be tomorrow? May each of our days be another step toward exaltation for ourselves and for those whom we have been sent to serve.

Love,

President Marbury

"Important principles may and must be inflexible."

—Abraham Lincoln

The Urgency Of Doing

Dear Missionaries,

   I have been impressed lately with the urgency of doing. Knowing is not enough. We must apply our knowledge. Willing is not enough. We must do.

   Progress is not created by contented people. It is up to us to be uncomfortable with complacency. It is up to us to refrain from being spectators and be players in the game of life. You are chosen by the Lord to perform a mighty work. You can do it because you desire it. May the Lord bless you as you serve Him. My wife and I love each of you.

Love,

President Marbury

"You cannot light a fire in another soul unless it is burning in your own soul."

—Harold B. Lee

USE TIME TO THE LORD'S ADVANTAGE

Dear Missionaries,

"All victory and glory is brought to pass unto you through your diligence, faithfulness, and prayers of faith" (D&C 103:36). We are competing with the adversary in a battle we cannot and must not lose. Three things are required for victory: diligence, faithfulness, and prayers of faith.

The diligent work smart. In every situation we should be asking ourselves, "How can I use this time to the Lord's advantage?" Stake conferences and other group meetings provide excellent opportunities. Missionaries, don't congregate together at a conference. Position yourselves throughout the congregation so that you may visit with the investigators and obtain referrals from the members. Sit with your companion and investigators or members, not with another set of missionaries.

The faithful live purely. Cultivate pure thoughts and dwell on those thoughts consistently. Each day, promise the Lord that you will serve him with all your heart, might, mind, and strength. Do good on purpose.

Prayers of faith require action. Pray as though everything depends on God. Work as though everything depends on you. In the mission field, we express our thanks by bringing souls into the kingdom of God. May we express our thanks abundantly.

Love,

President Marbury

"Today I will use my time to the Lord's advantage."

WHEN IN DOUBT—PRAY

Dear Missionaries,

"Be careful for nothing; but in everything by prayer and supplication with thanksgiving let your requests be made known unto God." (Philippians 4:6)

When in doubt—pray. We all know this; we just don't always remember. Stephen Van Rensselaer remembered. He was the senior member of the House of Representatives from New York during the presidential election of 1824. The popular vote was divided evenly, and it became the responsibility of Congress to decide who would become the next president. When all but Van Rensselaer had voted, the election was still tied. Van Rensselaer would cast the deciding vote. Seeking divine guidance, he closed his eyes, bowed his head, and reverently let his request be made known unto God. With head still bowed, he opened his eyes to see a discarded ballot on the floor. The ballot was clearly marked in favor of one of the candidates. Taking this as his answer, he voted, and John Quincy Adams became the sixth president of the United States of America.

The Lord will answer every righteous prayer. You are the Lord's righteous ambassadors. He loves you and will guide you as you let

Him. Ask and direction is yours—from One who knows the way. God bless you. My wife and I pray for you daily.

        Love,

        President Marbury

"When in doubt—pray."

WHERE SHALL I WORK TODAY?

Dear Missionaries,

Your diligence in keeping yourselves pure is uplifting as we watch you. Your desires to serve the Lord are apparent as you live the commandments, teach, and baptize. The Lord will reward you as you stay faithful.

I'm impressed by your desires to serve. Many have expressed a desire to be the best. I commend you for this. Sometimes many of you are concerned that you're not serving in what you feel are important positions. Please know that you are important and essential in your areas of service. The Lord has placed you where you serve because of the unique contributions you can make in your positions. Sometimes, often in fact, junior companions are placed with senior companions in order to teach the senior how to follow. Outstanding missionaries may not be called as zone leaders because they are the best suited and needed to train other missionaries. Aspirations for positions of authority can damage the spirit of the mission as well as the spirit of the missionary. As has been said so well by so many, "It doesn't matter where you serve, but how." This poem by an unknown author teaches a valuable lesson to us all:

Dear Missionaries

> "Father, where shall I work today?"
> And my love flowed warm and free.
> Then he pointed out a tiny spot
> And said, "Tend that for me."
> I answered quickly, "Oh no, not that!
> Why no one would ever see
> No matter how well my work was done,
> Not that little place for me."
> And the words he spoke, they were not stern,
> He answered me tenderly,
> "Ah, little one, search that heart of thine:
> Art thou working for them or me?
> Nazareth was a little place,
> And so was Galilee."

May the Lord bless you as you serve Him.

Love,

President Marbury

"Position doesn't save anyone, but faithfulness does."

Will You Give Up What You Are To Become What You Can Be?

Dear Missionaries,

You are a choice group of missionaries, chosen and loved of the Lord. My wife and I love you as our own children. You are achieving great victories. You can achieve even greater ones. Are you willing to give up what you are to become what you can be?

Moses, although born to Levite parents, was raised by Pharaoh's daughter. He could have been King. He was great in many ways. His destiny, however, was not to be king. It was to be a prophet. To fulfill this greater destiny, he gave up his rights as an Egyptian and took his place as one of the children of Israel.

Saul was a well-educated Roman theologian. His status as a Roman citizen entitled him to be treated with respect and dignity. As he was, he was almost guaranteed wealth and prominent social status for his entire life. His destiny, however, was to be a special witness for Christ, an apostle of the Savior. He gave up the former for the latter.

Jesus Christ was the God of the Old Testament. He had rank, status and position in the celestial kingdom. To become the Savior of the world, He had to give up His status as a God, for a season, and become a man. He had to be born in a stable and suffer the most agonizing of deaths. He gave up what He was to become what He could be.

You are missionaries, called of God to preach the gospel. Can you do that by simply doing the minimum asked of you? Your destiny is to be a savior to those in your area who have not yet accepted the fullness of the gospel. You do this by losing yourselves in the work; by sanctifying yourselves through prayer, obedience, and hard work; by reaching above and beyond the minimum requirements of an ordinary missionary. As you do ordinary things in extraordinary ways, you become what you can be. God grant you to do it.

Love,

President Marbury

"Are you willing to give up what you are to become what you can be?"

The Word Is Urgency

Dear Missionaries,

In remarks made during a regional representative seminar on April 5, 1976, President Spencer W. Kimball, a prophet of God, said this:

> Our objective is to bring the gospel to all the world. Some move toward their work as though they had all time and eternity to convert a few people in their part of the world. The word is urgency...It is now.

President Kimball has prayed,

> Oh, our Father in Heaven, bring about the day when we may be able to bring in large numbers, as Ammon and his brother did. Thousands of conversions, not dozens, not tens, not ones—thousands of conversions. The Lord has promised it. He fulfills his promises...May we improve the efficiency of our missionaries, each bringing thousands of converts into the Church.

Those of you who love the Lord, may I suggest these questions for you to ponder?

To whom is the prophet referring when he states, "Some move toward their work as though they had all time and eternity to convert a few people in their part of the world"?

Perhaps each of us is guilty of procrastinating our calling to be a friend to those who are still waiting to hear and accept the gospel. Perhaps some even say, "Why friendship and baptize them this week? They will be equally good members next week." We each have been instructed by the prophet to prayerfully select a nonmember family to friendship, to become their friend, and to invite them to share in the blessing of the Church. We are then instructed to ask the missionaries to teach them in our homes so that they may prepare themselves for baptism. If you have no one you are now friendshipping, is the prophet referring to you?

What does the prophet mean when he says, "The word is urgency—it is now"?

Familiar to all is the saying "Don't put off until tomorrow what you can do today." In the work of the Lord that means "Don't put off until tomorrow those who are ready to be baptized today." Of course, in order to be ready, the investigator must have gained a testimony, attended church meetings, and committed to live the commandments. It is our responsibility to help this process proceed as quickly as possible. The sooner our friends are baptized, the sooner they can receive the gift of the Holy Ghost. The sooner, also, they can receive the priesthood of God with its blessings and added opportunity for service.

Did President Kimball mean us when he asked Heavenly Father to allow us to convert numbers as Ammon and his brother did?

Of course he meant us, and we can do it. Dedication and love result in blessings from the Lord. A prophet has asked the Lord to allow us to baptize thousands, as Ammon and his brother did. He didn't ask the Lord to require us. He asked the Lord to allow us. If we desire it, if we work for it, it will happen. The Lord has promised it. He fulfills his promises.

How can we be a part of the fulfillment of President Kimball's prayer that we bring thousands of converts into the church, as the prophet requested of the lord?

The answer is a simple one. Follow the counsel of the prophet. Motivate members to have nonmember families taught in their homes on a regular basis. Avoid the phrase "Don't baptize unless...." Rather than being primarily concerned about why individuals should not be baptized, develop a concern to baptize every soul. When interviewing for baptism, remember that the Lord will hold new converts accountable if they are baptized unworthily because of their failure to speak the truth. The Lord will hold us accountable if we refuse baptism to those who are worthy or fail to help those not yet worthy to soon become so.

My wife and I love you all. We love all of the people living within the boundaries of this mission and throughout the world. No finer people live on Earth than those of you with whom we have been privileged to work. Our prophet's prayer for thousands of conversions will be answered. May we be righteous enough to be a part of the answer to President Kimball's prayer, I pray in the name of Jesus Christ. Amen.

Love,

President Marbury

"The word is urgency—It is now."

—President Spencer W. Kimball

Yes Virginia, There Is A Santa Claus

Dear Missionaries,

I thought you might like this letter by a young girl to *The Sun*, a New York City newspaper, which was sent in 1897. Here is it and the reply:

Dear Editor:

I am eight years old. Some of my little friends say there is no Santa Claus. Papa says, "If you see it in The Sun, it's so." Please tell me the truth; is there a Santa Claus?

—Virginia O'Hanlon
115 W. Ninety-fifth Street

***

Virginia, your little friends are wrong. They have been affected by the skepticism of a skeptical age. They do not believe except they see. They think that nothing can be which is not comprehensible by their little minds. All minds, Virginia, whether they be men's or children's, are little. In this great universe of ours man is a mere insect, an ant, in his intellect, as compared with the boundless world about him, as measured by the intelligence capable of grasping the whole truth and knowledge.

Yes, Virginia, there is a Santa Claus. He exists as certainly as love and generosity and devotion exist, and you know that they abound and give to your life its highest beauty and joy. Alas! How dreary would be the world if there were no Santa Claus. It would be as dreary as if there were no Virginias. There would be no childlike faith then, no poetry, no romance to make tolerable this existence. We should have no enjoyment, except in sense and sight. The eternal light with which childhood fills the world would be extinguished.

Not believe in Santa Claus! You might as well not believe in fairies! You might get your papa to hire men to watch in all the chimneys on Christmas Eve to catch Santa Claus, but even if they did not see Santa Claus coming down, what would that prove? Nobody sees Santa Claus, but that is no sign that there is no Santa Claus. The most real things in the world are those that neither children nor men can see. Did you ever see fairies dancing on the lawn? Of course not, but that's no proof that they are not there. Nobody can conceive or imagine all the wonders that are unseen and unseeable in the world.

You may tear apart the baby's rattle and see what makes the noise inside, but there is a veil covering the unseen world which not the strongest man, or even the united strength of all the strongest men that ever lived, could tear apart. Only faith, fancy, poetry, love, romance, can push aside that curtain and view and picture the supernatural beauty and glory beyond. Is it all real? Ah, Virginia, in all this world there is nothing else real and abiding.

No Santa Claus! Thank God! He lives, and he lives forever. A thousand years from now, he will continue to make glad the heart of childhood.

—Francis Pharcellus Church

May you all have a harvesting Christmas.

Love,

President Marbury

"Yes, missionaries, there is a Santa Claus."

Final Letter From Mission President To Full-Time Missionaries

Dear Missionaries,

This will be my last letter to you as your president. I'm grateful for you and what you have accomplished. You have set new records of accomplishment and dedication. You are the Lord's anointed and worthy to be called the sons and daughters of God.

I have given much thought and prayer to what my last counsel to you would be. It is this: Keep working on love. The real success in missionary service and in the service of our Heavenly Father comes through love. We are all here because of our love for the Savior. Sometimes in the rush and pressure of things we forget. Let all your decisions be made in love. When any controversy occurs between any of you, won't you resolve it in favor of the Savior? Love means sacrifice, among other things. If you're asked to do anything, please don't let personal, selfish desires rob you of the blessings that come through sacrifice in the service of Jesus Christ.

Sad, but true, you will not be loved or even treated kindly by many. Christ's counsel in these circumstances was,

> Love your enemies, bless them that curse you, do good to them that hate you and pray for them which despitefully use

you, and persecute you; that ye may be the children of your Father which is in heaven... And if ye salute your brethren only, what do ye more than others? Do not even the publicans so? Be ye therefore perfect, even as your Father which is in Heaven is perfect. (Matthew 5:44, 45, 47–48)

Thanks for being who you are. As one stake president, President Orlo W. Stevens, said, "We're not perfect yet, but the Lord isn't through with us either." My wife and I love you with all of our hearts. You will always be in our hearts and in our prayers. We hope we will always be in yours.

Love,

President Marbury

"Keep working on love."

Final Letter From Mission President To Stake Missionaries

Dear Missionaries,

This is my last letter to you as president of your mission. You have all been a great inspiration to me, and I thank you for your kindness and example during the last three years. The mission of the Church is to proclaim the gospel, perfect the saints, and redeem the dead. No one is doing these things better than you. With your example you have taught me that success is based on a positive attitude, unyielding courage, and warmhearted spirituality.

POSITIVE ATTITUDE

Can't is false doctrine in the Church. Jesus Christ told His apostles, "If ye have faith as a grain of mustard seed, ye shall say unto this mountain, remove hence to yonder place; and it shall remove, and nothing shall be impossible unto you" (Matthew 17:20). As you resolve to do anything, you will do it. During the Great Depression, Fred Allen and his partner lost their fortune. His partner committed suicide by jumping out of a window. Fred Allen became a millionaire and one of the most popular comedians in the Golden Age of Radio by traveling across the country telling jokes about the depression.

A positive attitude is a happy, persistent attitude. There are rewards for persistency in the work. A smiling stake missionary asked his friend if he wanted to know more about the Church. His friend answered, "No." Pleasantly, the stake missionary responded, "That's okay but be ready; I'll ask again."

UNYIELDING COURAGE

"For God hath not given us the spirit of fear; but of power, and of love, and of a sound mind" (II Timothy 1:7). Courage is of God. Fear is of Satan. If you persist in your fear, it will drive out your faith in Jesus Christ. If you persist in your faith in Jesus Christ, it will drive out your fear.

Decisions determine destiny; therefore, learn to make some decisions only once. As you make the decision to serve valiantly in the Lord's kingdom, have the courage to hold fast to that decision when the clouds are darkest. Develop the tenacity to finish. Where there is commitment, the Lord will compensate for any weakness.

It has been said that one of the great blasphemies of the Church is lip service. Have the courage to act. A little help will take the place of a lot of sympathy. The smallest act is more important than the best of good intentions. Develop commitment. Be determined to perform those services that everyone can but usually doesn't. Maintain the attitude, "I will not be average." Think big. Act now. As Sterling W. Sill said, "The pace that kills is a crawl." We will have all eternity to admire our labor, but only until sunset to complete it.

WARMHEARTED SPIRITUALITY

Warmhearted spirituality is our greatest tool in missionary service. Milkshakes win more friends than buttermilk. Runners, golfers, swimmers, and all top athletes train hard and regularly to perfect their athletic ability. If you desire to develop spirituality, you must put as much into it as the athlete. It takes conscious

Final Letter From Mission President To Stake Missionaries

effort to change one's thinking from, "I don't want to do this," to "the Lord wants me to do this, so I'll do it." It takes practice to govern one's actions every moment by the principle, "What would Jesus do?" Loving those who do as we wish them to do is easy. Spirituality comes as we love and understand those who act otherwise. The closer we come to Heavenly Father, the more we are prone to look with compassion on the weaknesses of others.

Never rationalize with the Lord. We cannot become perfect by imperfect means. To become like Christ, our value system must become like His. We must seek what is right and do it. To believe a thing and not do it is not honest. Spirituality comes through personal purity. Anything impure will insulate us from the Lord, and the adversary will never leave us alone if we give him the slightest chance. There are many ways to fail the test and only one way to pass. If you're not closer to your Heavenly Father, who moved?

Thank you again for all you taught me by your example during the last three years. Your example has resulted in a tremendous number of converts joining the Church each month. One activity survey of 3,195 new converts who were taught in member homes showed that 73.3 percent continue to be active. Even more impressive is that this same survey showed that of those who were immediately given positions in the Church, 97.1 percent continue to be active. My wife and I will never forget you. You will always be in our prayers, and we hope we will always be in yours. We love you all.

Love,

President Marbury

"We're not perfect yet, but the Lord isn't through with us either."

—Orlo W. Stevens

MORMON TRAIL CENTER
AT HISTORIC WINTER QUARTERS

Made in the USA
Lexington, KY
21 July 2013